THE GEEK'S GUIDE
TO DATING

THE GEEK'S GUIDE TO DATING

by Eric Smith

QUIRK BOOKS

PHILADELPHIA

Library of Congress Cataloging in Publication Number:
2012953989
ISBN: 978-1-59474-643-7

Printed in the United States of America
Typeset in Kongtext and Futura
Designed by Katie Hatz
Illustrated by Kickpixel
Production management by John J. McGurk

Quirk Books
215 Church Street
Philadelphia, PA 19106
quirkbooks.com

10 9 8 7 6 5 4 3 2

For Miguel Bolivar, Patrick Cassidy, Dario Plazas, Tim Quirino, and Michaelangelo Ilagan. For all those many days and nights filled with nothing but . . .

- ➤ StarCraft
- ➤ Diablo
- ➤ Halo
- ➤ Goldeneye
- ➤ Magic: the Gathering
- ➤ Pokémon
- ➤ *Lord of the Rings*
- ➤ Call of Duty
- ➤ *Futurama*
- ➤ Final Fantasy XI
- ➤ Reading GamePro
- ➤ Gears of War
- ➤ *Star Wars* and *Star Trek*
- ➤ World of Warcraft

. . . all while talking about girls. This, my friends, is for you.

CONTENTS

Welcome, Player One

layer One, I don't want to lie to you. Not at the very beginning of this book, nor at the middle, nor the end of it for that matter. This isn't *Portal*, and I'm not going to tease you with promises of cake. Within this playfully illustrated, reference-laden tome lies a true challenge. An epic quest that will lead you through the perilous, occasionally disaster-filled world of modern dating. It's a world as dangerous as Ceti Alpha V, confusing as *Crisis on Infinite Earths*, and challenging as the Special Zone levels in *Super Mario World*.

Dating has changed. The art of writing long, heartfelt "I *like* like you" letters has been replaced by the hookup sext message. Thanks to Google and Facebook, the blind date doesn't really exist anymore. Longing flirtatious stares are going by the wayside, as people become more comfortable with sending an ellipsis in a chat window. And with online dating becoming the new normal, concepts like courtship and chivalry have started to feel somewhat dated.

There have been days that I, much like the aging gamer who clings to his original Game Boy with its fading screen, have yearned for simpler times. For the days of old when one could hop into a chat room on America Online, type in *A/S/L?*, and immediately find a soul mate. For a time before Facebook poking and direct messaging on Twitter, when getting your crush to notice you required talking face-to-face, or at least passing them a note along the lines of *Do you like me? Circle Yes or No.*

As a lovesick kid, I always tossed a *Maybe* in there, just to spice things up a bit.

So how do you date in a world where people, to some extent, don't really date anymore? Where they become close virtually rather than in person, via texts instead of over dinner? Where a phone call to say how you'd really love to see them tonight, or a long pause before asking someone to come upstairs, is replaced with a text that says "… sup? ;-)"

By embracing traditional rules, and staying old-fashioned in a modern world. Or, better yet, updating those traditions for the modern age.

Technology and the gadgets we've been blessed with have certainly made life easier and taken us in the direction of making all of Gene Roddenberry's wildest dreams come true. But as much as modern tech and the Internet have made the world feel a little smaller, they've also managed to push us apart. You don't need to look all that far for proof.

I mean, there's an app called FaceTime just for face time.

As a kid, I projected myself into video games (as I once described in detail in the online literary journal BygoneBureau.com). When playing an RPG, I always renamed the characters when given the option. In *Chrono Trigger*, I was always Crono. His best friend, Lucca, was renamed Darlene, after a girl who's been my closest friend since I was 8 years old. Robo, Frog, Ayla, and Magus have been given an array of names over the years—always for the people closest to me. And Crono's love interest, Marle? I named her after various crushes and, later, different girlfriends. During a play-through on my iPhone, as I renamed Marle after my current sweetheart, it hit me: this nearly two-decade-old RPG about time travel has been with me through all of my romantic relationships. And it's taught me valuable lessons about being brave (Crono goes after and saves the girl), learning to accept yourself (Robo is accused of malfunctioning, of being broken), not giving up on love (Robo doesn't find his match until after he transcends time), and moving on from the past (Frog recovering from the disgrace of letting down Queen Leene).

Technology, games, fantasy worlds, superheroic characters . . . I love them all. I'm a still-sometimes-awkward 30-year-old man who owns a Master Chief suit and plays *Chrono Trigger* on his iPhone, and I'm okay with that. Because I use technology as a tool, not a crutch.

See, there's a reason why we geeks always read the book, graphic novel, or comic series before seeing the movie. Why we acknowledge the original series before checking out the reboot. Why we take the time to play with Magic: The Gathering cards and Warhammer 40,000 figurines before trying out the various video game adaptations. Honoring tradition, understanding the way things originally were—and why—makes embracing modern ideas even better. The same principle applies whether we're talking about remakes of *Battlestar Galactica* or about meeting that special someone. In this book, we'll explore the lessons embedded in the pixels and codes and equations and datastreams of the geek canon. Old-school lessons about love and relationships, honor and allure, heartbreak and loss. Lessons that have stood the test of time (and time travel).

What this little book is going to challenge you to do, Player One, is to upload traditional dating rules into the operating system of the modern dating world. This quest will challenge you. It will upset, infuriate, and frustrate you. But like all good quests, if you undertake it for the right reasons, the experience is its own reward. Your journey is about to begin, Player One. And on that journey, I wish you luck.

It's time to press Start.

Player One,

PRESS
START

CHAPTER 1

Selecting Your Character: Your Quest Begins

ood to see you, Player One. Grab a spot on the couch; help yourself to those chips and some Mr. Pibb. (I know, you wanted Pepsi, but Mr. Pibb was on sale.) We'll bust out some beers later on; for now, you'll want to keep a clear head.

So, we both know why you're here. You're tired of living life in single player mode; you're on a quest for a Player Two to call your own. Maybe you've already tried to recruit a partner at a local tavern or cantina but ended up flying home solo. Maybe you've yet to make a first move in the three-dimensional chess game that is dating. First off, relax. Sure, you're eager to start the search for your smizmar. But Rome wasn't built in a day—not even Space Rome, where Kirk, Spock, and McCoy fought in the gladiatorial arena. Before you saddle up and ride towards adventure with map in hand and longsword sheathed over your shoulder—even before you spend some precious silver pieces on torches, daggers, and a ten-foot pole (to check for trapdoors)—you have to spend a little time assessing your stats and checking your skills.

Here's the thing, Player One: It is incredibly important to get to know yourself and figure out what you want before you start dating.

Otherwise, you're just going to end up wasting time. Example: Most of the drama that the characters in the Final Fantasy series go through could be avoided if only they knew who they were and what they were looking for. True, that drama makes gaming interesting, but IRL who needs the aggravation? (And even as a gamer, you could have skipped a lot of dungeon crawling and level grinding if you only knew that—spoiler alert!—Tidus in *Final Fantasy X* was a dream.)

Think of the classic heroes of the geek canon: James T. Kirk. Han Solo. Batman. Each of these guys is successful in whatever he puts his mind to—whether exploring uncharted galaxies, smuggling stowaways out from the Empire, or fighting for guerrilla justice in Gotham—because, ultimately, his quest comes from a deep, personal conviction that's rooted in his identity. That's what makes them so awesome, so confident, and that's why we like them. And while the characters you encounter in the dating world are (hopefully) not as sleazy as Jabba the Hutt or as Arkham-insane as the Joker, you still need a strong sense of self to see you through. It's just like the Oracle in *The Matrix* told Neo: "Know thyself." (Okay, maybe Socrates said it first, but the point remains.)

So before we start talking dating, let's start talking *you*. Let's assess your strengths and weaknesses, figure out where in the dating realm you should plant your flag, and—because this chapter is all about boosting your confidence to John Constantine–type levels—we'll use those traits to engineer you into an awesome, unstoppable, dating machine.

A Note for the Gal Geek

It goes without saying, though I'm saying it anyway, that geeks come with XX chromosomes, too. So if you're a geek girl reading this and wondering whether this book is for you, the answer is yes . . . with qualifications. Much of the info-dump in these pages is written with the guy geek in mind. But lots of it is equally applicable to women, whether it's identifying your particular geek subtype (page 26), making conversation (page 41), planning a date (page 87), or dealing with the aftermath, whether good or bad (page 147). We're long past the days when a girl couldn't ask a guy out, after all. You may need to make some gender-specific tweaks—skip the section on facial hair—but I'm confident you can handle that. As for the specifically male subject matter, there's value for you there, too. It's a window into the male geek mind, a glimpse of the obstacles he has to double-jump over to reach you. Maybe you could lower the difficulty level a bit? (But not too much . . . he's gotta *earn* that high score.)

What Kind of Geek Are You, Anyway?

Being a geek means a lot of things, Player One. The definition is constantly evolving. What was once a derogatory term for a socially inept person has now been taken back by a community proud to wear the title. A community comprised of people just like you and me. We're eccentric, enthusiastic, intelligent, and, occasionally, kinda awkward.

But we're also *especially well-prepared for dating*. That's right, I said it, and here's why: When you get past the labels, a geek is first and foremost fiercely passionate about something specific. Whether it's comic books, video games, movies, or the latest gadgets, a proper geek has a passion he is consumed with, likely to the point where it becomes a serious part of his lifestyle. (Lady geeks: please excuse my use of the male pronoun throughout; you can rest assured that a majority of my sweeping generalizations about geeks apply equally to you. See also "A Note for the Gal Geek," opposite.)

Good news for us geeks: this capacity for passion is a total plus when it comes to the dating experience. It means we're loyal, chivalrous, creative, and great at remembering even the most seemingly trivial of details—all of which are Very Good Things in a relationship. And the reappropriation of the geek identity into the hands of geekdom means that "geek" doesn't automatically stigmatize us as someone who's shy and awkward (but for those who are—don't sweat it, I've got your back too).

Your particular geeky passion is something to keep in mind when looking for a new love interest. Obviously, if you find someone who hails from the same Class M planet that you do, you'll have lots of common ground on which to build a relationship. But don't let your passions trump your destiny. Yes, chances are that if you absolutely adore comic books, dating someone who *despises* them might not be the best idea. On the other hand, if you keep an open mind, you may find that the two of you have other attributes in common: mutual disdain for the "first" three *Star Wars* movies, perhaps, or an adoration for obscure indie rock, or a conviction that fast zombies aren't really zombies at all. Exceptions can be made, so don't close the pod bay doors too soon. Love, like nature—and please read this with Jeff Goldblum's *Jurassic Park* voice—*will find a way.*

Knowing your geek type will also help you suss out your strengths (and weaknesses!) for dating. So let's take a look at the different kinds of geeks, figure out which one you are, and determine the strengths, weaknesses, and special abilities of your particular character class. Here you'll find them broken down into three key categories: Pop Culture Geeks, Technogeeks, and Academic Geeks, with the strengths, weaknesses, and special abilities typically found within each phenotype. Special abilities are ranked in relation to their frequency in the general human population: +1, above average; +2, superior; +3, highly superior.

GEEK SPECIAL ABILITIES LIST

As a geek, you possess plenty of admirable qualities that are sorely lacking in most normals. To help you identify your special abilities (so you can use them for good, like Hal Jordan, not evil . . . also like Hal Jordan. Remember when he became Parallax? Don't be that guy. You won't be able to redeem yourself by reigniting the sun.), here's an inventory list of the gifts and capabilities commonly found in the geek gene pool. Then read about the different types of geeks on pages 26–33 to figure out which of these tools are most likely to be found in your particular utility belt.

Communications officer: There was a time—back in the First Age, perhaps—when geeks could only share their lore in person, via letter columns, or by—gasp—*land line*. But these days, electronic communication allows us to practically Vulcan mind meld at will. Geeks with this talent know how to share ideas and maintain social connections through multiple channels: via text, Skype, IM, blogging, social media, online communities, and (someday soon, we expect) subspace carrier wave.

- **Use this talent to:** Spark a romance online (see Chapter 2); keep a relationship going between dates; get dating advice from a variety of contacts.
- **Don't use this talent to:** Overwhelm her with neediness; invade her privacy; bug someone who's made it clear she's not interested. LeChuck is notorious for this in the *Monkey Island* games. Though as an undead pirate, I doubt he had the means to use any form of modern communication.

Curator: All geeks collect, but the curator knows how to *choose*. If you have this ability, you're able to sift through the dross and spot the best. Whether it's a flood of titles on new book Wednesday, or a sea of websites all purporting to be the next BoingBoing, you zero in on the good stuff and don't waste time with the zeroes (except Mega Man Zero, Monster Zero, the ZeroZone, Hero Zero, and Dimension Zero).

- **Use this talent to:** Choose a gift that matches her interests and inclinations; introduce her to the best examples of your own interests; help her prioritize her pop-culture choices.
- **Don't use this talent to:** Criticize the books, movies, TV shows, etc., that she likes; rearrange her Netflix queue; avoid trying out new stuff that she suggests. Do not ever "Comic Book Guy" her. ("Worst. [Noun]. Ever.")

Deep thinking: Due to prolonged exposure to heavy scientific concepts or wildly speculative fiction, you've developed a capacity to go beyond facts, numbers, and equations (as beloved as those may be) and see the *implications* they have for the world, the universe, reality itself. Others see the trees, a geek with this trait sees the whole forest moon of Endor.

- **Use this talent to:** Engage her in thoughtful, philosophical conversations; draw surprising connections between the trivial and the cosmic; encourage her to share her dreams and aspirations.
- **Don't use this talent to:** Make yourself seem all-knowing; avoid making small talk; denigrate other people's lack of scientific literacy. Some people like real science. Others love Michael Crichton. Both are fun.

Empathic sensor: Thanks to immersive experiences that put them inside the minds of a wide variety of characters, some geeks excel at understanding the motivations of others. What would you expect from someone who role-plays a scheming vampire one day, helps Kratos avenge his family the next, and then engages in a fiery debate over the motivations of mutant superheroes feared and hated by those they've sworn to protect?

- **Use this talent to:** Display an understanding of her point of view; express genuine pleasure at her successes and accomplishments; tell stories about people in your life.
- **Don't use this talent to:** Tell her what she's thinking; assume that your guesses about other people's behavior are always right; dissect and diminish her emotions. Emulate the traits of good telepathic characters, like Abe Sapien and Professor X, and resist the urge to be like Loki or Aquaman. (The second

example isn't evil, you just shouldn't waste your time talking to dolphins.)

Minutia recall: Stats, facts, rules, secret identities, scientific principles . . . every geek carries around an assortment of these in his head. Being able to retrieve them when you need 'em, though, is a skill not all geeks possess.

- **Use this talent to:** Reference a surprising statistic to spark an interesting conversation; remember her birthday, favorite color, and other relationship-sustaining details; connect with her on topics you're both interested in.
- **Don't use this talent to:** Spit out numbers and factoids like you're some kind of Vulcan-robot hybrid; show off your knowledge of obscure subjects she doesn't care about; prove that you're always right.

Money master: Some geeks manage to parlay their talents into unlimited money, like, say . . . Bill Gates. But for most of us, our obsessions tend to exceed our budgets (hey, those comics come in *every week*). A geek with this talent has mastered the art of squeezing every last copper piece until it begs for mercy, all the better to keep the game shelf full and the lights still on.

- **Use this talent to:** Plan spectacular outings on a limited budget; demonstrate your fiscal responsibility; come up with thoughtful gifts that are more valuable than their price tag.
- **Don't use this talent to:** Criticize how she spends her money; veto any expenditure of cash that's beyond your comfort level; inconvenience her so you can save a few nickels and dimes.

Sense of adventure: You spend hours virtually questing for . . . well, you name it. You seek out films whose plots are incomprehensible even after they're subtitled in English. Do these things enough, and inevitably a craving for new and different experiences will bleed into your RL world. That weird restaurant with the unpronounceable menu items, the new club that hosts bands nobody's ever heard of, the aloof girl in the coffee shop who's always scribbling in her notebook—to you, they're mysteries to be solved.

- **Use this talent to:** Make her feel that you can find magic in the most humdrum of situations; plan surprising and unforgettable dates; turn an unexpected obstacle (wrong turn; closed restaurant; orc attack) into an interesting experience.
- **Don't use this talent to:** Criticize her for wanting to do something "normal"; avoid responsible behavior (like showing up on time and planning ahead); put the two of you in unreasonable jeopardy.

Solutionizer: In the mundane world, few problems can be solved by, say, shoving big blocks of stone around to raise an iron grate. Nevertheless, geeks who spend lots of time pondering solutions to virtual or theoretical problems can develop a knack for MacGyvering their way out of real world dilemmas, too. Sometimes a brainload of technical or scientific know-how facilitates this trait; other times, it manifests itself as a dogged refusal to give up until a creative solution is found.

- **Use this talent to:** Help her figure out how to get all her errands done with a single car trip; improvise a toy for her cat using the stuff lying on the coffee table; fit all the dishes in her dishwasher without blocking the flow of water and soap.

● **Don't use this talent to:** Attempt to repair something of hers that you can't actually repair; micromanage every aspect of your date; tell her and everybody else that they're doing it (whatever it is) wrong.

Tech know-it-all: A certain level of comfort with technology is a geek hallmark (and, let's face it, a must for anybody who wants to get anywhere in the twenty-first century). With this trait, however, you can move quickly past the stock answer of Roy from *The IT Crowd*, "Have you tried turning it off and on again?," and get to the root (or root directory) of most electronic glitches.

● **Use this talent to:** Fix her computer, phone, e-reader, and iPod—if she asks you to; advise her on purchasing electronics and gadgets; teach her how to correct technical problems—if she doesn't already know how.

● **Don't use this talent to:** Make changes to her electronics without permission; be snobby about her lack of tech-fu; resist learning from her if she knows more than you do. (And if she knows Shaq Fu, skip ahead to "Boss Level" on page 179.)

Wide-open mind: It's a human instinct to be put off by the strange, the different, the unknown. But it's a geek instinct to prefer those things to the ordinary, the same, the predictable. A geek with this trait never judges a book by its cover, whether the book is a shrink-wrapped anime DVD with a large-eyed kitten-headed ninja on the front, or an alluring neighbor with a weird accent and a peculiar haircut.

● **Use this talent to:** Demonstrate your fair-mindedness; share strange and unique experiences that you've had; introduce her to new concepts and ideas.

- **Don't use this talent to:** Prove how cosmopolitan and unusual you are; one-up her anecdotes with stories of your own; scare her away with weird interests before she really gets to know you.

POP CULTURE GEEKS

The great thing about pop culture is that it makes geeks out of everyone. And why not? There's a lot to love (and ship, and fanboy over) in the world of comics, movies, and TV. Several kinds of geeks fall into this category, each with their own unique passions. Which one are you?

The Comic Book Fan

Strengths: Whether you refer to your collection as graphic novels, *manga*, or plain old comic books, you likely have a certain set of noteworthy characteristics. You have a strong imagination (kind of a requirement when your favorite characters die, come back, travel to alternate dimensions, become zombies, etc.). You're patient (waiting for the next issue ain't easy) and fiercely loyal, a champion of the characters and series that you've been following since comics cost less than three bucks.

Weaknesses: You can be overprotective (sure, *Action Comics* #1 belongs in a glass case, but most things—and people—will be just fine if they are not quite in mint condition). Sometimes you're too defensive (this comes from having to stick up for that one obscure character that you love but all your friends hate). And, let's admit it, you do tend to be overcritical (in comics, writers and artists change projects at the drop of a hat, so there's always someone who "did it better.")

Special abilities: Curator +3, Minutia recall +2, Money master +3

The TV & Film Geek

Strengths: If you're this kind of geek, you're likely a romantic. Special effects and lens flares are great, but ultimately it's the relationship arcs of the characters that draw you in (admit it—you're still totally shipping Mal and Inara). You also have a great memory. You remember the important things: the first date, the first kiss, the first song that Fry learned how to play on the holophoner in that episode of *Futurama* (like I said, the important things!) Apply this to your anniversary, your girlfriend's birthday, and the names of all of her friends, and you're sitting pretty.

Weaknesses: Despite all the CGI, film and video are inherently more real-seeming than other types of media. So remind yourself that life rarely occurs with structured story arcs, supporting characters who lack motivations of their own, and a tidy resolution in ninety minutes or less. And a word of warning to the letter-writing types who campaign for new seasons of shows spurned by the networks: Relationships aren't like *Jericho* or *Family Guy*. When they're done, they're done, and no amount of complaining on the Internet will bring them back.

Special abilities: Sense of adventure +2, Empathic sensor +3, Minutia recall +2

The Gamer

Strengths: Like comic book fans, you gamers are dedicated and loyal, but you're also seekers of novelty (after all, even MMOs like World of Warcraft get stale without patches and expansion packs). If you're a gamer, you're constantly questing and leveling up, a competitive instinct that suits the thrill of the chase in the dating world.

Weaknesses: The flip side for you as a gamer is a tendency to conflate girls IRL with your virtual damsels in distress. Think of girls more like NPCs: they're the quest *givers*, not *rewards*. Better yet, consider them as co-players: it's the two of you against the world, if you can just find a way to be on the same team.

Special abilities: Empathic sensor +1, Sense of adventure +3, Solutionizer +2

TECHNOGEEKS

Geeks and technology go hand in hand (or hand in . . . mouse?). In any case, even within the geek community there are those whose facility with the technological makes them practically wizards. After all, we all know what Arthur C. Clarke said about technology and magic.

The Internet Geek

Strengths: Memes. YouTube videos. Animated .gifs. Social media. Blogs. You know how to use the 'net to find out cool new things—which gives you the upper hand when it comes to everything from planning first dates to keeping a relationship fresh. It's important to you to keep up with what's going on in the world around you, so you'll likely have plenty to talk about with that special someone. And you enjoy preserving all the little moments, whether they're special (a first date) or not (a poorly lit photo of the sky over Williamsburg with the contrast turned way up). Like Paul Bettany as Chaucer in *A Knight's Tale*, you take an active part in recording the history unraveling before you. And hopefully, you're just as charming.

Weaknesses: Your future dates shouldn't expect to enjoy that romantic dinner before you've scanned Yelp for the best restaurant, found a deal on Groupon, and then taken a nice picture of the meal and shared it on Instagram. Which is fine, but there's a point at which digitizing your life can interfere with experiencing your life, Player One. So be willing to dial back on the blogging and downloading and feed reading so you can enjoy real life in real time with a real person.

Special abilities: Minutia recall +3, Tech know-it-all +2, Wide-open mind, +1

The Apple Geek

Strengths: The typical Apple geek isn't afraid to spend a lot of money on the latest, greatest iteration of some handheld gewgaw he already owns. Translation in the dating world: you're not afraid to sink a lot of time/money into something (or someone!) if you truly feel they are the best. +1 Fidelity! If you're among this exclusive cohort, you appreciate intuitive, friendly interfaces and attractive, eye-catching design. You like to keep things simple and prefer to avoid drama and complication. And you have a heightened sense of style, an eye for the finer things—when it comes to electronics, at least, and perhaps for design as well. Try to keep as stylish and put-together as the latest iPhone. Remember always: Wozniak was the exception. Jobs was the rule.

Weaknesses: Sometimes a rush to own v11.0 makes you forget how much you love v10.7.5. The grass isn't always greener on the other side of the fence, so appreciate what you have before deciding to chuck everything and go after what seems better—whether it's a nicer phone or a new girlfriend. Also, nobody likes a snob. Putting down others whose tastes aren't as discerning as yours won't earn you any likes from your lady, Player One (unless she's also a snob, in which case, please don't have kids).

Special abilities: Tech know-it-all +1, Money master +1, Curator +2

The PC Geek

Strengths: While Apple geeks might spend loads of loot on the latest shiny product, a PC geek is the sort to just build it himself, piece by piece. As a PC geek, you're patient. You like knowing how things work, and you play close attention to detail. And this is a great trait to have when dating: everyone loves getting attention, and a burning desire to engineer things efficiently will serve you well in fine-tuning your love life (as will knowing how to put the RAM in, *if* you know what I mean).

Weaknesses: It's great to be a problem solver, but be careful not to be *too* reductive about it. Remember that, technically speaking, people are *not* machines. Interacting with the humans can be a squishy affair, and not just literally. Not everything that people say and do makes logical sense, and not every human problem has a logical solution. And here's something to keep in mind: not everything *you* do will seem logical to the woman you're trying to get to know, no matter how rational it seems in your own head.

Special abilities: Tech know-it-all +3, Solutionizer +2, Money master +1

The Social Media Geek

Strengths: The social media geek might not necessarily be obsessed with the actual Internet. If you're one of these, you prefer the channels that *connect* you to it. You're on Facebook, Twitter, Tumblr, and any other virtual sharing gadget that lets you interact with other people. As the name suggests, social media geeks crave interaction with others and value keeping in touch with a wide circle of people, which is a double-edged vorpal sword of sorts. On the plus side, this makes you more comfortable and skilled than most geeks at communicating your thoughts, ideas, and opinions to others. You can cut through the clutter and get your point across. On the other hand . . .

Weaknesses: . . . if you're not careful, you'll cut yourself off from people who want to spend time with you. The trick is converting your tendency towards poking and @replies into actual convos in meatspace. And, like the general Internet geek, you may have trouble unplugging for undistracted face-to-face time (as opposed to FaceTime). Master the art of friendly conversation on- *and* offline for maximum results (for more on dating and social media, check out Chapter 3).

Special abilities: Communications officer +3, Tech know-it-all +1, Wide-open mind +2

ACADEMIC GEEKS

If you're an Academic Geek, you probably don't collect as much as the Comic Book Geek, Apple Geek, or any of the Pop Culture Geeks, although you undoubtedly have several shelves full of well-organized volumes on your area of specialty. Not to mention an armoire devoted entirely to lab coats . . . or maybe that's just me. No, the real basis of your collection is in the mind, and you're more likely to be into someone based on a solid conversation or a glimmering intellect than anything else.

The Book Geek
Strengths: You love to read—obviously. But you've also got a lot of excellent traits. Besides being well read, you as a book geek are often a great conversationalist, creative, and good with words. You can parlay this into dating by engaging a woman in deep conversation instead of the excruciating small talk that she so often has to endure from normals. Find an interest of hers and draw on your knowledge to hold your own in a free exchange of

ideas (and, hopefully, phone numbers). Better yet, hit the library to deepen your knowledge of the topics she's into and then dazzle her with your expertise.

Weaknesses: If you're a bibliophile, your eyes will immediately dart to the bookcase when you walk into someone's home for the first time. You know you're not supposed to judge a book by its cover (as it were), but you can't help it. You're only human (unlike the protagonists of the *Twilight* box set you're casting your judgey glance on). Instead of treating someone's taste in reading matter (or lack thereof) as a red flag, use it as a jumping-off point to ask questions that go deeper than the usual get-to-know-you fare. Hey, maybe there's some redeeming value to the *Twilight* series that you've overlooked. (Spoiler: There's not.)

Special abilities: Curator +1, Empathic sensor +2, Wide-open mind +3

The History & Politics Geek

Strengths: Geeks who enjoy politics tend to be well informed and opinionated. Your love for facts and research will help you get to know people beyond the surface—and you aren't afraid of a good, friendly argument, either. And, most admirably, whatever your party affiliation may be, you *care* about what's going on your country and your world, and you aren't afraid to search for solutions.

Weaknesses: Academics tend to be more interested in intellectual theory of politics than picking apart the spittle-flecked rhetoric du jour, which is great. But even though you're smart enough to avoid today's hot-button issues in small talk, take care not to go too far to the obscure side, either. Adam Smith's theories of political economy might be a lot safer than Glenn Beck's, but they're also a lot more boring.

Special abilities: Communications officer +1, Deep thinker +1, Minutia recall +2

The Math & Science Geek

Strengths: If you're into equations and concoctions, you really do understand the world around you. You're well focused, curious, skeptical, and devoted to the scientific method. Good news: experimentation works in the social world, too! Conduct experiments (Hypothesis: If this girl laughs at a periodic table joke, she is awesome. Results: Affirmative!).

Weaknesses: Just keep in mind that the heart is more than an organ that provides blood circulation through the cardiac cycle. No equation can calculate love (feel free to borrow that line for a Valentine's card), so you'll have to get out of the lab and into the field. Remember that some questions aren't meant to be answered literally, or at all. (Examples: "What are you thinking?" "Do you think she's prettier than me?" "Does this make me look fat?")

Special abilities: Deep thinker +3, Solutionizer +1, Wide-open mind +2

Knowing Is Half the Battle

Not to go all G.I. Joe on you, Player One, but you know what they say about knowing stuff: it's, uh . . . responsible for at least fifty percent of your success.

Fortunately, since you're a geek (and since you've just read and absorbed all that handy info above), you already know a lot. All you've got to do now is wrap your head around how your vast, impressive nerd knowledge can be channeled into getting the girl . . . and I'm here to help with a few more key bits of information. Call this next part the *other* half of the battle.

IT'S A TRAP! THREE MYTHS THAT WILL BUST THE GAME

Even if you haven't been dating much, or at all, you probably have *some* idea in your head of what you're looking for. And maybe you're waiting for that dream girl to cross your path before you make a move. Or perhaps you already are dating; friends keep setting you up, you're futzing around on online dating sites and meeting folks at the local pub . . . and your ideal woman just does not seem to exist in this continuum. Why can't you find her?

Player One, your instincts are correct: the woman you're look-ing for *doesn't* exist. You're the victim of a non-Jedi mind trick, the result of years of movies, video games, comic books, and television telling you she's out there and available. You're trapped in a Matrix of delusions, but I'm about to feed you the red pill. So follow me down the rabbit hole as I reveal the top three misconceptions about women that are likely causing you trouble in your search:

The Princess Problem

You've quested with Link, shot fireballs with Mario, and traveled back in time with Crono, all for the same purpose:

To save the princess.

Since the sacred era of the 8-bit game, we've been assaulted with scenarios that tell us women need saving. That in the event you find a damsel in distress, you should make a move and be a hero. Here are the two main problems in this situation:

- **She's not an actual princess.** Unless you run in the same circles as royal families, it's not likely you've found a real live princess. Even if you have, she probably doesn't need to be rescued. You want to date the woman, not save her.

- **The nice guy isn't always so nice.** More often than not, if you try to sweep the girl off her feet in rough times you come off more creepy and desperate than chivalrous. Be a real hero to women everywhere, and don't be that guy. And by the way, if she constantly leaving you messages that she's in another castle . . . she's just not that into you. Move on.

The MPDG Dilemma

After watching Cameron Crowe's *Elizabethtown*, film critic Nathan Rabin coined the term Manic Pixie Dream Girl (MPDG) to describe Kirsten Dunst's character. He explained that an MPDG is a "bubbly, shallow cinematic creature that exists solely . . . to teach broodingly soulful young men to embrace life and its infinite mysteries and adventures."

This character archetype isn't limited strictly to movies, though it is certainly easy to think of almost endless examples in mainstream cinema, like Penny Lane in *Almost Famous* or Sam in *Garden State*. There's Ramona Flowers from Bryan Lee O'Malley's brilliant Scott Pilgrim series and Charlie ("the answer to all the world's problems") in Nick Hornby's *High Fidelity*.

Here's the thing, Player One. As much as this concept has been romanticized, it neglects the fact that women are human beings with their own issues—they don't exist just for you. If you're considering finding yourself a MPDG, stop. Become a whole person. You should never pursue a relationship because you're looking for someone to fix you. Just as it's not about saving the woman, it's also not about the woman saving you.

The character of Clementine in Charlie Kaufman's film *Eternal Sunshine of the Spotless Mind* says it best: "Too many guys think I'm a concept, or I complete them, or I'm gonna make them alive. But I'm just a fucked-up girl who's looking for my own peace of mind. Don't assign me yours."

The Impossible Standard Deviation

I get it, Player One. You've spent a lot of time watching flawless women in *Battlestar Galactica* (I was totally crushing on Number Eight) and looking at wildly proportioned females in comic books. These images may be beautiful and vibrant, but real people aren't shaped that way. And if they are, they are likely structurally unsound and need to visit a doctor immediately.

As a result of entertainment marketed towards the geek community, we've all been given some seriously impossible standards of what a woman should look like. But you can't expect RL ladies to look like fictional characters played by actresses and enhanced with CGI, SFX, perfect lighting, Photoshop, and body doubles. For example, very few healthy women have a waist that's smaller than a normal person's neck. If you yourself don't inspire comparisons to guys like He-Man and James Bond, imagine how normal women feel about being compared to She-Ra and Pussy Galore.

In the *Big Bang Theory* episode "The Vengeance Formulation," Howard Wolowitz confesses he thought he'd settle down with someone more like Megan Fox from *Transformers* or Katee "Starbuck" Sackhoff from *Battlestar Galactica* than Bernadette, the girl he's currently dating. Later, a fantasy version of Sackhoff explains that her real boyfriend is tall, handsome, and rich, and that Howard should be out with a wonderful girl like Bernadette who cares about him, instead of wasting his time fantasizing.

Howard learns a valuable lesson that we can all benefit from: Hold potential love interests up to an impossible dream standard, and you could miss out on something great that's right in front of you.

PARALLEL REALITIES: DO YOU ALWAYS DATE THE SAME TYPE?

How many times have your male friends fallen for someone emotionally unavailable? Or your female friends complained that the person they're a smitten mess for has commitment issues? It's likely you've heard this several times, over and over again from the same person, because they've slipped into a pattern they can't quite escape from. There's a danger in putting your dating life into repeat mode, Player One. Narrowing your horizons in any aspect of life, whether we're talking about career, education, or love, is a bad thing.

And there is, of course, the constant risk of making the same mistake over and over again.

So as you enter, or re-enter, the dating realm, take care not to turn into that guy who makes the same mistake over and over again. Do you really want to be Bill Murray in *Groundhog Day*?

Okay, maybe that's a bad example, because Bill Murray is awesome, and ends up with Andie MacDowell, and you probably just said yes to that question. But you get the idea. As charming as Bill Murray is, no one wants to make the same mistakes again and again, starting over from scratch each time. Remember, although weatherman Phil Connors initially enjoyed knowing exactly what each day would bring, his circumstance eventually became a living nightmare. He made it past the endlessly repeating cycle only when he changed his shallow, smarmy ways and forged a true connection with Rita.

Or consider Ash, in Pokémon (we'll mention *Evil Dead* Ash another time). His Pikachu has more personality than any of the other Pokémon in the whole Pokémon universe, so it's no surprise that the li'l yellow guy is his go-to pocket monster. Occasionally, Ash needs to use a Pokémon other than his favorite, yet he usually doesn't until poor Pikachu has had his electric butt handed to him. Sometimes we choose to date the same type of person again and again because we find it comfortable, easy, and familiar. And when it goes wrong, we wonder why. So don't choose Pikachu every time, Player One, no matter how cute that lighting-bolt tail may be. Try a Squirtle or a Charizard and see what happens.

REBOOT, OR SAVE AND CONTINUE? LESSONS IN SELF-REINVENTION

No one is perfect, Player One. And in the geek canon, it's usually the characters who are outside the norm—those with extraordinary gifts and questionable quirks—who deal with the greatest inner turmoil. They struggle to be accepted not just by society, but by potential love interests (sometimes I think there are more broken hearts in comic books than there are character deaths and resurrections).

Change can be good—evolution ain't just for Pokémon, after all. But there's a difference between changing your costume and trying to rewrite your whole origin story. How many times have comics readers seen a "new take" on a familiar character completely erase everything that made the character cool and interesting in the first place? How many character reboots have alienated fans so much that the writers had to find a way to bring back the classic version?

Longtime comics readers can easily name a slew of characters who struggled to come to terms with their issues and eventually found a way to accept themselves. The same story arc is popular in other forms of pop culture (not to mention serious literature, but that's a different story). You can do the same. Here are some examples, both success and failures, that we can all learn from.

Dr. Horrible: Poor Billy. His pursuit to reinvent himself includes becoming a supervillain, joining the Evil League of Evil, and finally defeating Captain Hammer. Just as he wants to change himself, he wants to change all of humanity. Unfortunately, this gets in the way of the pursuit of his love interest, Penny, a bright-eyed, sweet woman who dedicates her time to helping people less fortunate. In the end—spoiler alert!—Dr. H gets what he wants . . . but loses the girl in the worst way possible: he accidentally kills her.

The Lesson: Let this be a warning, Player One—leave death-ray building to the professionals, or your potential girlfriend could *die*. More realistically, trying to hide who you really are will likely blow up in your face, possibly killing a romance before it begins.

The Thing: Of all four of *The Fantastic Four*, Ben Grimm is definitely the least fantastic-looking. Reed Richards, Susan Storm, and Johnny Storm all got to stay human-ish and dress in sexy, form-fitting outfits while nevertheless acquiring superpowers. Ben? Dude is a giant hunk of orange-colored rock in blue shorts.

Ben struggles with his appearance throughout the series, his angst sometimes amplified by brief reversions to humanity. But eventually he comes to realize that he's more than just his looks. Over the years, Ben manages to develop relationships with a number of women in spite of his monstrous appearance, including Alicia Masters, Debbie Green, and Sharon Ventura, better known as Ms. Marvel.

The Lesson: A craggy exterior isn't a dealbreaker. Keep trying, and you'll find someone who can see the hero underneath.

Steve Urkel: In the classic '90s sitcom *Family Matters*, we're introduced to Steve Urkel, an awkward teenager who represents just about every geek stereotype you can imagine. After years of trying and failing to win the affections of his neighbor Laura Winslow, Urkel invents a serum called "Cool Juice" that transforms him into his ultrasuave alter ego, Stefan Urquelle.

It works, for a while. Stefan and Laura even get engaged. But the transformation is doomed to fail. Stefan is self-centered and pompous and vain. In the end, Laura asks him to turn back into Steve.

The Lesson: There are no shortcuts to change. Trying to cover your faults with a fake personality just makes you seem shallow. Better to be honest about your flaws and work to improve them, and find someone who appreciates you warts and all.

Beast: Hank McCoy of the Marvel universe had a rough time growing up. A mutant blessed with huge hands and feet, he was referred to as Magilla Gorilla by his classmates. Eventually, his self-image took an even bigger beating when he transformed into the furry blue werewolf/cat-looking creature known as Beast.

But does he let all of this get him down, or embark on a rampage against those stupid humans? No. He goes on to become a political activist and uses his genius intellect to inspire change and take down monstrous, godlike superbeings. Oh, and Kelsey Grammer played him in the third X-Men movie (that's less a spoiler alert and more a *warning*).

The Lesson: Work with what you've got! Shake what your mama gave you. When people draw the wrong conclusions about you because of superficialities, there's nothing sweeter than proving them wrong.

Barnell Bohusk: Also known as Blackwing, Bohusk, much like Beast, had a tough childhood. Having been picked on and nicknamed Beak due to his fledging-chick-like appearance—his face a mess, his arms like wings—he eventually enrolls at the Xavier Institute, is taken under the wing of Beast, and joins the X-Men.

As he becomes more sure of himself, Bohusk becomes involved with and falls in love with fellow mutant Angel Salvadore (later known as Tempest). While this relationship begins because of a dare (isn't that how so many romantic comedies start?), it eventually blossoms into something genuine. The couple has children, they get an apartment together, and frankly, it's one of those rare comics relationships that doesn't end in epic disaster.

The Lesson: Put yourself out there, even though you're not perfect. Bohusk was far from the most confident, charismatic, or human-looking mutant around. But he pushed himself past his comfort zone, which created an opportunity to click with Angel and, eventually, live the life he'd always wanted.

FEEL THE FEAR AND TALK TO HER ANYWAY

It goes without saying that starting to date is a lot like leading a raid in Upper Blackrock Spire in *World of Warcraft*.

Okay, if you're not a WOWer, I suppose it goes *with* saying. Here's what I meant: When it's the first time you've ever done it, leading this raid is hella intimidating. Hell, if it's the *zillionth* time you've ever done it, it's still intimidating. Knowing that you are responsible for everything going right, and that the slightest move can attract too much aggro, is enough to either paralyze you or make you go totally Leeroy Jenkins and get everyone wiped.

If there's so much potential to screw up—in front of your group of guildies to boot—then why even try?

Well, obviously no one's going to force you to slay dragons. But no one will ever force you to screw up the courage to start talking to a girl you like, either. That's the thing: You're the one with your hands on the controller. And you're the only one who can push yourself out of your comfort zone.

The good news is, in dating, as in WOW, you will always resurrect from a bad encounter, with only a little bit of invisible armor damage and no reason not to try again. Take a few minutes, re-equip your best gear, and wait for a respawn. And remember, no matter how bad you *think* you did: at least you have chicken.

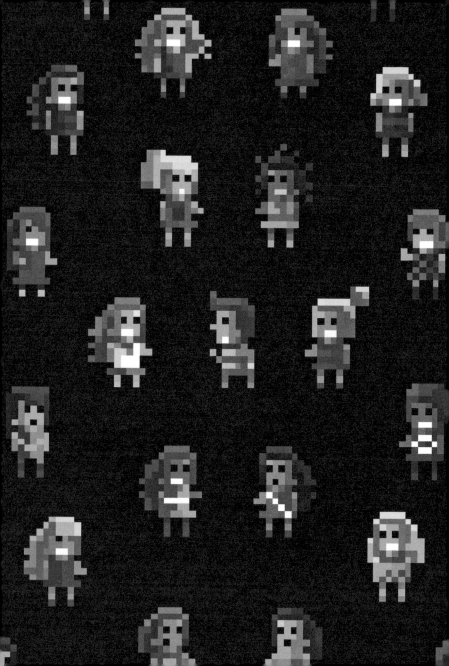

CHAPTER 2

Engage! Plotting Your Course through the Dating Realm

s Alan Moore pointed out in the excellent *SMAX* miniseries (a spin-off of his also excellent *Top 10* comic), questing in real life is much harder than it's made out to be in stories. In a book, the questing party wanders around for a paragraph or two, you turn the page, and *bam!*, there's the cave with the dragon, the gold, the damsel in distress, and a legend-spawning battle ready to start up. In real life, your quest for Player Two may sometimes feel like a bit of a slog.

Patience, Player One, is a virtue (and, in some gaming systems, as critical as a rulebook and a set of dice), so don't give up the search. I'd hand you a map if I could—one with a clearly delineated trail that bypasses forests, graveyards, and fire swamps infested with Rodents of Unusual Size—but I can't choose your path for you. What I can do, in this chapter, is guide you into the same hex as your damsel—and give you some opening moves that will get you two on speaking terms. Then, in Chapter 3, I'll prep you to Release the Kraken. (By which I mean ask her out . . . get your mind out of the gutter, Player One.)

And here's good news: as a geek, you have access to not one but *two* worlds that may contain your soon-to-be-significant other. We'll begin with the digital one, since you can survey the online scene from the comfort of your own Fortress of Solitude.

Greetings, Programs: Online Dating and You

Meeting potential mates IRL isn't easy for everyone. But we geeks are lucky to have numerous online channels available for us to connect with and meet people with similar interests: MMORPGs, social media outlets, and the most popular and common of the bunch, online dating websites.

From niche sites aimed at specific wants and desires to mainstream sites that cater to a general audience, there's a seemingly endless array of options out there. Of course, not every one of those channels is premium. To quote the knight from *Indiana Jones and the Last Crusade*, "You must choose, but choose wisely."

Big-name sites like eHarmony and Match.com are flashy, well known, and full of promises. That said, they also charge fees and tend to attract a more settled (read: marriage-minded) crowd—which is great if that's what you're going for. But a slew of cheap and free sites are aimed at the young and technologically savvy (read: you, Player One): OkCupid, Plenty of Fish, How About We, *The Onion* Personals, and Reddit4Reddit are all worth checking out. (There's Craigslist, too, but something about that bare-bones layout just screams "buyer beware.")

Like subatomic particles, new dating and matchmaking sites are popping in and out of existence all the time. So instead of trying to give you the lowdown on each frakkin' one of them, I'm going to equip you with some general principles that you can use on whatever dating site you like. Note: while these kinds of websites are, by design, places where people arrange to date, your social networking platform of choice—Twitter, Facebook, or Friendster if you somehow fell into a time warp—can also connect you with a possible Player Two. After all, these are places where people regularly communicate with one another and reveal information about themselves. You and the object of your affection may even have connections in common. (Of course, asking someone out over social media presents special challenges, which we'll cover in Chapter 3.)

HOW TO HACK YOUR ONLINE DATING PROFILE

Writing a profile for a dating website isn't quite like building your avatar in *World of Warcraft*, or writing a clever Twitter bio, Player One. For one thing, it doesn't have to take nearly as long to get right. For another, if you do it right, the payoff is much more satisfying—but don't let that make you obsess. Like any system designed for efficiency, online dating is totally hackable.

Step 1: Hack your user name. Your online moniker (along with your profile picture; more about that in Step 2) is the first glimpse of you that other site users get—which means it's your first chance to catch someone's attention. Remember how much time you put into coming up with your Xbox Live user name or your Twitter handle? You should put just as much thought into this alias. Do you really want to be another LongDong69 or CuteBoi32? Of course not. You're a geek, and as a geek, you're creative.

Give yourself a username that says a little something about you and your personality: maybe it's a character in a comic (Gambit42), the title of a book you enjoy (RdyPlyerOne), or a play on a (nonembarrassing) nickname of yours.

Think carefully before picking a name that can connect you to your IRL self. Avoid using your Twitter handle, your Facebook username, or your real name: you don't want your dating profile popping up when a potential employer Googles you. By the same token, you don't want your whole personal life showing up when a potential date Googles you. So stay off the radar, and keep your identity a secret, instead of shouting it out to the world.

Step 2: Hack your photo. First of all, choose pictures that are of *you*, without anyone else in the shot, so you'll be clearly visible in the thumbnail. Secondly, if the site supports it, post a handful of images—you don't want to imply there is only one good photo of you in existence. Finally, be sure to choose recent photos. Surprising your date with the fact that you lost all your hair . . . well, that's not good. You should never start a relationship with a lie.

The best practice is to take a couple of fresh pictures especially for your dating profile. Surveys of OkCupid user data show that successful pictures (i.e., the ones that attract the most messages) have a few things in common that are easy to put into practice:

- **Better camera, better picture.** Users with photos from a DSLR camera were more successful than those with point-and-shoot pictures, who were in turn more successful than those with camera-phone snaps. Borrow a great camera if possible (and if you are stuck with a phone-cam, try to use an iPhone—surveys show iPhone users have more sex).
- **Flash no, natural light yes.** Popping that flash can add almost seven years to the appearance of your face. Turn off your flash and stand outside or by a window (late afternoon is best).
- **Be shallow.** In your depth of field, anyway. Use a low f-stop on your camera when possible or, in layman's terms: keep your

- face in focus, with the rest receding to a soft blur. Or use the "portrait" setting if your camera has one.

- **Don't look at the camera . . . or even smile.** It sounds counterintuitive, but guys whose pictures show them staring resolutely offstage make contact with nearly twice the women per attempt than the deer-in-headlights grinners. But try to go for mysterious and thoughtful, not creepy and crabby.

If you want to pull something from your photographic archive instead of booking a photo shoot, here are some examples of good shots you probably already have:

YES	NO
You, dressed well and looking nice.	You at a party chugging down cans of beer or tumblers of whiskey like you're Wolverine or Tony Stark.
You sitting outside at a restaurant, glass of wine in hand.	
	You at home, shirtless in the bathroom mirror, in your boxers, etc.
You at home, sitting on the couch, cooking in your kitchen, posing with a pet, etc.	
	You sitting outside at a restaurant, mouth full of meat, bones scattered across the table, spoils of war everywhere, none spared. If you look like a zombie extra from *Shaun of the Dead*, it's probably a bad choice of picture. (Unless you actually *were* a zombie extra—that could be cool. Just make sure you explain that clearly in the caption.)

Please, please avoid the "glamour shots" (by Napoleon Dynamite's girlfriend or anybody else). And by no means should your portrait have lasers in the background, no matter how ironic.

Step 3: Hack your "About Me." You've got to be honest. Boasting about being the world's strongest millionaire might work for Bender in *Futurama*, but if you're trying to find something long term and lasting, it's best not to lie. (If you are in fact the world's strongest millionaire, you definitely don't need this book, but thanks for picking it up anyway!) Here are some cheat codes for getting the truth across painlessly.

- **Standard playthrough:** "I'm looking for a Droid to man my battlestation/a Penny to my Dr. Horrible/a Princess Peach to my Mario."
- **Cheat code:** "I'm a laid-back guy looking for an awesome girl to share adventures with."

The battlestation was blown up. Dr. Horrible accidentally kills Penny. And Peach is constantly running around other people's castles. That is to say: avoid clichés and avoid hiding behind fictional characters. Be original and genuine . . . unless you truly do love piña coladas and getting caught in the rain. In that case, good luck with the pneumonia and alcoholism.

- **Standard playthrough:** "Well, the first thing to know about me is that I was born in California, but then spent my whole life in Seattle, which means that I've been to Emerald City Comicon three times: once in 2008, once in 2009, then not again until 2011, and then I thought about going in 2012 but I ended up deciding to try for PAX tickets until they sold out, so I ended up having to throw together a costume at the last minute . . ."

- **Cheat code:** "I'm from Seattle, which means I've got my pick of awesome cons to attend."

It's not easy to condense your life story into a few sentences, but fight the urge to pen a *Lord of the Rings*–length epic about yourself. Most dating websites give you room to rant and ramble, but in the age of Web 2.0 and mobile browsing, lots of potential dates are checking out your profile on their smartphones. Provide just enough intriguing details to give them a good idea of who you are. You can cover the rest in person on that first date.

- **Standard playthrough:** "I've had zero luck dating in meat-space and I'm trying this as a last resort, but I bet girls online are just as harsh and stuck-up as IRL."
- **Cheat code:** "I'm an online dating n00b. Who wants to show me how awesome it is?"

Yes, relationships are tricky, and when things don't work out, you may be left jaded and cynical. But if that's your opening line, why would anyone want to hear more? Don't be like Rorschach in *Watchmen*, writing down all his sad, painful thoughts. Keep the negativity off your profile.

- **Standard playthrough:** "I'm pretty into movies, music, video games, etc."
- **Cheat code:** "I love *Lord of the Rings* and have watched the extended editions of the movies back to back. Twice."

This is probably the most important tip regarding the content in your dating profile: don't hide your true self. If you're afraid to admit that your ideal weekend consists of playing Dungeons and Dragons or that you obsess daily over the possibility of a zombie/robot apocalypse, don't sweat it. If it sends someone running, chances are she wouldn't have been right for you anyway. Let your geek flag fly, because *someone* will salute it.

- **Standard playthrough:** "Not looking for anyone younger than 21, older than 25, taller than me, or unable to speak Klingon. No redheads, no 'drama,' no fat chicks."
- **Cheat code:** "Are you funny, smart, and willing to laugh at my jokes? I'm sold."

There's a difference between knowing what you want and providing a horribly long list of what you don't want. Pre-jecting people with an itemized list of unwanted flaws means you might miss out on someone truly awesome because of one small quirk, and you'll definitely make yourself look like a person with impossibly high standards—aka a tool.

- **Standard playthrough:** "im just tryna find the right girl 4 me atm"
- **Cheat code:** Spellcheck. Every time.

You may think typos and grammar gaffes make you seem more casual and relaxed. Or maybe you just suck at spelling. But dating sites have found that illiterate profiles get lower response rates. Spellcheck obsessively, and ask someone you trust to proofread your profile.

 If you have a friend who uses the website you're signing up for, ask her or him to take a look at your profile and offer feedback.

 If you're looking at other people's profiles for inspiration, *stop*. You want to stand out. Make your profile as unique and interesting as you are.

OPEN HAILING FREQUENCIES

As science fiction has proved time and time again, making first contact is tricky. Sometimes things go well and you make a connection that leads to a free exchange of ideas (or DNA). Other times, your ship goes down in flames and you end up being captured and . . . examined.

So once you've spotted a life form you'd like to know better, how do you make sure your first contact is pleasant, like *Batteries Not Included*, and not horrific, like *Independence Day*? Think of the plaque on the Pioneer spacecraft: there's a map, a diagram of the hyperfine transition of hydrogen, and a friendly picture (okay, yes, it's a naked picture, but it's acceptable there because this is science). It's short and to the point—which is the best way to avoid sending mixed signals. Here are some simple guidelines for posting your opening message.

Alo? Salut. Don't just say "Hey." Pick something a little more unusual. One survey found that messages that kicking off with a jaunty "How's it going?" get almost *two and a half times* the responses of ones with a puny "Hi."

Be friendly, not creepy. On OKCupid, complimentary adjectives like "cool" and "awesome" get nearly twice the response rate of physically focused words like "sexy" and "beautiful." In other words, focus on her personality, not on her looks. Read her profile and then keep your compliments grounded in what you've read—something about her as a person, her excellent taste in movies, books, video games, etc. Or try making friendly suggestions. Does she talk about loving a certain kind of food? Bring up a favorite place in the area. Is she wearing a T-shirt of an interesting band? Give her some music recommendations.

Proofread. As mentioned above, avoid netspeak—it's guaranteed to get you a rock-bottom response rate. Don't send out a message without double-checking it. And use real words; "Ur" "r" "u" and "ya" make it seem that you put no thought or effort into your message.

Be succinct. Your name isn't Robert Jordan and you're not writing the *Wheel of Time* series. Short and sweet, my friend.

ALL ISN'T FAIR IN LOVE & MMORPGS

In the virtual realms of Massive Multiplayer Online Roleplaying Games, you can be anyone (or anything). But sometimes slipping into the persona of your level 89 Orc Unholy Death Knight can actually make it easier to be yourself. And sometimes, when you're running quests and casting spells, you find yourself—your *real* self—falling for someone onscreen. I'm not talking NPCs here, Player One (you're on your own with your crush on Jaina Proudmoore)—I'm talking about a fellow player, guildie, or RP partner.

Communities in long-running flagship MMORPGs, such as *Everquest*, *Guild Wars*, or *World of Warcraft* encourage banding together and growing with your guildies just like a group of IRL friends. So you and your cute fellow player clearly have something in common—you like the game. But you've also got a lot keeping you apart—an entire virtual world sits between you and her. What's an Orc like you to do? Don't sweat it: a lot of the same principles for meeting and dating apply on both Earth and Azeroth.

Get some alone time together. "Massively multiplayer" doesn't have to apply *all* the time, after all. There are plenty of ways you can interact outside of your guild or party with your potential love interest without the distraction of other humanoids. Ask to go on a quest together, send some private messages, and get to know this person beyond her character. If your game has a voice chat function, take advantage and use it to make conversation—nothing intense, just something friendly to help pass the time while you're slaying dire wolf after dire wolf together. If she seems interested in getting to know you too, take that as a cue to make your next move. But if she spends all her time trying to get loot or turn in quests, chances are she's just in it for the leveling and epic drops. Respect that—after all, it *is* a game.

Look for positive signs. When your connection to her is an Internet datastream, the signs that she's into you are a little different than their offline counterparts. Examples include virtual gifts (she shares her swag), in-game mail (she drops you a line just to say hi, or sends you a whisper as soon as you log in), voice chat (talking to you—actually talking, not just shouting "need heals!" and "spam AoE spells *now!*" at each other—might be an indication that she's interested), and leveling for you (if she's helping you out, she's thinking of you).

Build trust. Whether it's something casual, serious, long distance, or virtual, every relationship needs trust. But trust isn't something that just happens. It's something that's earned, like when you fight with your allies in groups or raid parties. You need your teammates to heal you, cast protective spells, and stay on the offense while you defend against mobs, and vice versa.

So how does she act in those scenarios? When a boss threatens to overwhelm your entire party, does she stick it out or run away? Or, worse, does she just come back to pick up loot when the battle is over? If she seems prone to use you and your comrades as cannon fodder, be wary. (Chances are she's noting your behavior, too, so don't be a leech.) But if she seems trustworthy, then maybe it's time to . . .

Take things seriously—virtually. Before you take the next step and make thing serious IRL, try moving things forward in your virtual world. Spend extra time gaming together, get into real conversations about what you're looking for in a partner, and maybe even make your relationship in-game official—one researcher has found that 10 percent of male players and 33 percent of female players have been in MMORPG marriages (just don't become that obnoxious couple spamming the guild chat channel with mushy crap). As time goes on and you quest together more and more, you'll build up XP *and* trust together. And once you have, then you might be ready to . . .

Connect offline. No matter how great a connection might be, you need to have things in common outside the game. If that's the only way you connect, your relationship will grow stale quickly. It's time to try transitioning to other parts of the Internet (social media, Skype) or even plain old phone contact, and talking about your offline lives. If and when it's feasible, make a plan to visit one another—but include a backup plan in case things fall through, because if you meet up and things don't work out, you won't be able to just hearthstone yourself outta there.

Check for traps. As fun as MMO dating can be, there are some risks associated with gaming with someone you've got a crush on, including:

- **Trolls:** Trolling isn't just limited to name-calling and griefing. It can also mean leading you on, secretly badmouthing you in the guild, or using you—for loot or for laughs. It's cruel, and it's unusual, but it's just as damaging as stuff that happens IRL. Keep your guard up until she's earned your trust (and you've proved your trustworthiness to her).
- **Sock puppets:** There is always the risk that the person you

are talking to and falling for isn't who you think they are. Take care in getting to know this person. Remember, anyone can be *anyone* on an MMO, so keep your stranger-danger smarts around you.

Crashing and burning: Depending on how invested and intertwined your two characters are, a virtual realm breakup can be almost as complicated—and sometimes more so—than one that happens IRL. Who gets shared assets if your partnership dissolves? It's not like you can sign a prenup. Will there be fallout among your guildies? Don't make people choose sides; no one wants to be around the couple who gives new meaning to the phrase "the Sundering." If things don't work out, could you handle creating an entirely new character, switching to a different MMO, or even logging out of your virtual life for good? Ponder the issues before you plunge into a roMMORPGmance, Player One.

MMORPG Relationships in Pop Culture

Finding love via MMORPGs is a fairly common occurrence for characters in the geek canon. And luckily, there's a lot to be learned from a handful of examples therein.

Parzival and Art3mis: In Ernest Cline's (utterly brilliant) novel *Ready Player One*, we meet Wade Owen Watts, a young, smart gamer on a quest to unlock the ultimate Easter egg in the OASIS, a massively multiplayer online simulation game (think *Second Life*). Along the way, Wade (alias Parzival) meets Art3mis, a world-famous blogger, on whom he has a monster cyber crush. Art3mis makes it clear that there is a difference between who she is in game and who she is on the outside, and Parzival doesn't care. Good lesson: falling for someone in a virtual realm means falling for who they *are*, not what they look like.

Willow and Malcolm: In an early episode of *Buffy the Vampire Slayer*, the normally responsible Willow becomes distant. She misses classes, flakes on spending time with Buffy and Xander, and eventually goes a little crazy . . . all around the time she meets a boy named Malcolm on the Internet. Surprise! In traditional *Buffy* fashion, Malcolm in fact is a demon that Willow unleashed online from a library book, and he's trying to kill Buffy.

What can we learn from this?

One: don't let your love life get in the way of staying close to your friends. Two: make sure the person you're falling for isn't an ancient demon.

Howard Wolowitz and Glissinda the Troll: In season 4 of *The Big Bang Theory*, nerdy engineer Howard gets dumped by his girlfriend, Bernadette, because he is having an online fling with a *World of Warcraft* character named Glissinda, who turns out to be a creepy (male) sanitation worker at the university.

Lessons? One, don't cheat. Virtually messing around still counts, geeks. You shouldn't be pursuing any kind of romantic venture online if you're already involved with someone IRL. And two, as we discussed earlier, it's **very** important to know who it is you're talking to. So take the time to find out.

Codex and Zaboo: In the first season of Felicia Day's hilarious web series *The Guild*, we're introduced to Zaboo, a Warlock player who smitten with Day's online character, Codex. He becomes obsessed to the point that he shows up at her doorstep uninvited and acts like they're a couple.

This doesn't go well.

The takeaway? Gauge whether or not the person you're interested is reciprocating your interest. Codex clearly wasn't into Zaboo, but he didn't care. It causes a lot of conflict in that first season, not to mention it made him seem really weird. So if she's not interested, back off and you'll still have an excellent guild mate—no need to ruin that.

Welcome to Erf: Meeting Women in the Real World

"Being clever's a fine thing, but sometimes a boy just needs to get out of the house and meet some girls." Such is the wisdom of Flex Mentallo, wrestler/superhero/metafictional comic book character. He's advising the angsty teen who not only is Flex's creator but may also be on the verge of destroying reality and preventing a group of fictional superheroes from becoming real and . . . well, it's a Grant Morrison story, so let's stop there, before the metaphysics get too thick. The point is, Flex is right: the real world is the natural habitat of most women. (Jerry, in an early *Seinfeld* episode, points this out to George: "There's girls everywhere. . . . Look, look, there's one over there. Look, there's another one. Soon as I walk outside, there'll be girls out there.")

Now, you sure won't get any criticism from me for using the power of the Interwebs to search for a romantic partner; I think the previous section of this chapter makes that pretty clear. But, to put on the Spock ears for a moment, it's a matter of logic. If you don't also look for opportunities in the physical, nondigital world, you're significantly limiting your options. The real world is where women go about their business and, as every fisherman (and Aquaman) knows, you have to fish where the fish are.

Planet Earth is a big place, of course, even if it's not a gas giant or a Dyson sphere. So we're going to narrow our search parameters to a few key coordinates. But first, I want to share two important principles that you should keep in mind when mining for that heart of gold.

First: If you want to maximize your opportunities, it's very important to go questing off-map. In a study conducted several years ago, researchers used cell phone transmissions to track the movements of 100,000 people over the course of six months (the identities of the trackees were kept anonymous—so they say). The researchers found that people tend to spend most of their time visiting the same few places over and over again. Not exactly surprising, maybe, but think about what that means, Player One: the person you've been looking for might very well buy her coffee at Cup O' Joe's every afternoon, but you'll *never* meet her because you only patronize Caffeiney Meeny Miney Moe's, just across the street. Your mission: vary your routine. Every time you boldly go where you've never gone before, you're likely to cross paths with people you otherwise never would have encountered (because they never step out of their ruts either).

And second, you really should try to expand your social network—not in the Zuckerberg sense, but in the people-with-whom-I-interact-offline sense. Surprisingly, your best bet is to increase the number of *casual* friendships you have, instead of spending all your time with a small, close-knit group. The reason: people who you know well probably know all the same people that you do. But that guy who goes out for beers with your brother now and then? Or the dude two cubes down who eats lunch in the break room a few times a week? They're potential connections to whole new social networks—women included—if you just get to know them a bit better.

SEARCH OPTIMIZATION, PART 1: WHERE TO MEET GEEKS

Finding someone to date shouldn't be like trying to party up in an MMORPG: running around, repeatedly spamming chat channels for a group, and anxiously seeking a random encounter. (Random, casual encounters are for Craigslist. This isn't that kind of book.) No, seeking out Player Two is more like an old-school RPG: a gradual progression that, with the right walkthrough, becomes much, much easier.

So let's start with suggestions for traversing familiar terrain, places where you're almost guaranteed to find gals who share some of your geeky interests. Of course, these aren't the only places where geeks are found—we don't lurk only in niche locations. As mentioned, it's to your advantage to change up your routine; try the comics shop or video game store on the other side of town now and then. But, home quadrant or no, one of these locales is more than likely to harbor the fem geek of your dreams. And the next time she crosses your path, you'll know how to turn a chance encounter into a conversation.

The comic book store: Every one of your geek brethren wants to ask out the cute girl who turns up at the comic book shop. But keep your cool, Player One. Just because a girl joins you in freaking out over a model TARDIS or a signed, limited-edition comic book variant doesn't mean she wants to join you for coffee (after all, it's not like every guy you bond with over *X-Men* becomes your best friend). Plus, if the girl in question *works* at the store, what you see as playful flirting might just be her doing her job.

So take a breath, and don't present yourself as another drooling geek guy trying to land the only gal in town who knows the difference between the Phantom Zone and the Negative Zone. Here's how approach your geek store crush:

Observe the girl in question. The local comic book store is a bastion in your neighborhood geek community. If someone is shopping in there, she's got a geek card in her wallet. Is she browsing the new releases? Eyeing up the limited-edition collectible toys? Asking questions about an upcoming signing? Quickly assess her interests to have fodder for conversation. Don't take a long time, and don't stare; you're not Jack Bauer or Ethan Hunt, so eventually she's going to notice that you have her under surveillance.

Approach her. If she looks up as you walk over, make eye contact and smile. Don't hesitate—a lack of confidence will quickly mark you as creepy.

Break in with a question. Using the observations you've made about her interests, make a relevant query requesting her opinion, advice, or expertise. Hold back on your own opinions for now. Judgment might *seem* suave, but it's more likely to come off as condescending.

YES	NO
"It's cool that you're so into *shoujo* manga. What would you say is the best series to start with?"	"You don't seriously think that hearts-and-flowers crap is the same thing as a real graphic novel, do you?"

Start a conversation, not a debate. No matter what she says, react positively, or at least neutrally. Sneering at someone's taste is not a surefire way to getting a date. If you hold a different opinion, try to find some common ground.

YES	NO
"Yeah, I guess the special effects of *Episode I* were considerably better than Lucas's earlier work."	"You prefer the *prequels*? Are you blind or just stupid?"

 Comic book shops are a lot more than just brick-and-mortar establishments for finding your latest issue of *X-Men* or scoring collectable statuettes. They also serve as a social gathering place, especially on certain days. New Book Day (every Wednesday, when new releases come out) and Free Comic Book Day (the first Saturday of every May in the U.S.) are when geeks descend upon the local shops like a ravenous Galactus on a defenseless planet. In other words, these are great days to meet passionate fellow geeks. Plus,

Free Comic Book Day often falls on the same weekend as the opening of a major (geeky) motion picture. Instant date idea!

 If it's a clerk you've got your eye on, proceed with caution. If you make a move and she shoots you down, your favorite hangout may become an incredibly awkward place to visit. If you do connect but things don't work out, will you really want to keep shopping there if your ex will be at the register? Maybe yes, maybe no—just make sure you weigh the potential pros and cons.

The video game store: Dust off that second controller, Player One, and scope out the local video game shop. Just as with comic book stores, gamers can often be found at their local retailer when the new inventory arrives (most new console games come out on Tuesdays). And just like comic stores, there's plenty to talk about. The walkthrough is similar:

Observe. Is she buying or trading something? What's her console of choice?

Approach. Eye contact, smile, quick nod hello. If she seems put off, abort mission to avoid lurking.

Speak up. Again, try to solicit her expertise on something. No geek girl *doesn't* like being asked her opinion.

YES	NO
"Okay, if you had ten bucks of trade-in credit, which game would you buy?"	"Please tell me your favorite game isn't actually *The Sims*."

 Want to find the most passionate of video gaming geeks? Head to a midnight release party. It's a magical time when geeks wait in line to be among the first to score a copy of the latest blockbuster title. With luck, you'll end up standing near someone who has nothing to do but wait around and talk to you.

 If the store has a demo game system set up, challenge her to a round of whatever's on. Turbocharge it by making it "winner picks a date location."

 Don't judge a gamer by her choices, even if she's buying a "bad" game. The same way you wouldn't judge a music or movie fan for liking one guilty pleasure song or film, you shouldn't brush off a gamer just because you catch her picking up the latest piece of shovelware or critical failure. Keep an open mind.

The arcade: Arcades are another great venue to meet geeks who are truly passionate about their niche. Here, you'll often find more mature, adult geeks: the ones with a sense of nostalgia, who appreciate the past, but hopefully don't *live* in it (unless it's the world of Frogger, circa 1982. That would actually be kind of cool, if you could avoid getting crushed.). While they're gathering places primarily for the "Remember When" crowd, remember that new games continue to come out. Here's the launch sequence:

Don't delay. The advantage of an arcade is that it's hard *not* to notice what a girl's doing (playing a game, duh), so you don't have to invest too much time in figuring out what she's into. Read the side of the console and you're good to go.

Challenge her to a friendly bout. This is a no-brainer for a 2P game like *Mortal Kombat*, but it can also work for a single-player game. If she's button-mashing at the helm of *Ms. Pac Man*, offer to take turns and get a wager going on who can eat the most delicious, delicious dots. And depending on the game, you may find yourself in the only actual situation appropriate to the phrase "on like Donkey Kong." As always, if she's not into it, be polite and move on.

Keep the momentum going. Win or lose, the end of Round 1 is a great time to invite her to try another game with you. A quick, friendly chat in between consoles can also be a great lightning-round get-to-know-ya. Just don't be patronizing about it.

YES	NO
"You seem like you're more of a *Soul Calibur* than *Street Fighter* type. Want a round two?"	"How about a second chance to beat me? I'll go easy on you this time, promise."

 There's a growing trend of arcade/bar combinations. See if you've got one of these hotspots nearby. At such hangs, there's a good chance you'll find a geek who isn't just into gaming, but also knows how to be social . . . unless she's just there to sip PBRs while playing Joust.

 Arcades can be a male-centric environment, so watch out for accidental sexism. If you're playing, say, *Galaga*, at your favorite gaming palace, don't go easy on your female opponent "because she's a girl." You're just wasting her time. She's there to play the game! And she might just kick your behind.

The bookstore: Whether you're at a used bookshop, a quirky indie, or a major chain, bookstores are a great place to browse for your dream geek. Here's how to play follow the reader:

Assess the aisle. What's she interested in? You might spot her browsing through the new releases or thumbing through the science fiction/fantasy section. Maybe she's picking up a paranormal young adult novel or checking out the classics. Take note!

Use your words. Even more than the other venues we've discussed, a bookstore is a place where people of widely varying interests come together. Geeks buy and read books of all kinds, so there's a good chance that she's checking out something you're unfamiliar with. Ask her about the book—just don't try to sound like an English professor.

YES	NO
"I've been meaning to try the *Silmarillion*. Do you have to know the original trilogy to understand it?"	"Ah, yes, *The Joy Luck Club*. Finally, a novel that marries a literate examination of the relationships between mothers and daughters with the complex, multifaceted narrative of immigrant experience in America."

 Again, don't judge someone based on her selection. We've all picked up a Tom Clancy or Nicholas Sparks book once in our lives (though hopefully it was an accident). And maybe that copy of the latest Danielle Steele hardcover is for her mom.

 Reversing this move and making your own suggestions can also work well. If she's picking up the latest George R. R. Martin, ask her if she's ever read Robert Jordan. Just don't react with hostility if she rejects him—or you.

The convention: Comic Con, video game expos, anime conventions . . . these are tricky places to navigate. Maybe that good-looking cosplayer just wants to hang with her friends and be left alone. That lady rummaging like mad through the dollar comics? Maybe she *could* use a tip on where to find vintage issues of *Astro City*—but if she's on a quest, you might just be another annoying NPC. Plot your course carefully, and follow this flight path:

Make a plan of attack. Good news: If you're looking to meet someone at a convention, the epicenter of geekery, the con schedule may include events centered around doing just that. From geek speed dating to networking events, many conventions offer a plethora of opportunities for single fanboys and fangirls to socialize one another.

Get some one-on-one time. Whatever your context for matchmaking, try to talk with a girl without anyone else leaning in to offer his opinions (or to distract both of you). Speed dating events make this easy. In less structured situations, try to position yourself so your back is towards any potential interrupters, blocking their field of vision. (Don't do anything that invades her space or makes her feel trapped, though. You're not Kraven the Hunter.)

Don't lurk or linger. Sure, asking for a picture of the girl in the handmade Card Captor Sakura outfit is an easy way to start a conversation, but chances are guys have been hitting on her all day. So if she doesn't ask for further contact, don't push it. Cosplayers are there to dress up, take pictures, and hang out with their like-minded friends—not humor pallid fanboys who try to get all stalkerish on them. Don't be "that guy" (and definitely no hover hands!).

Use a strong offense. She's at a convention. You're at a convention. In other words, both of you are geeks. So don't feel shy about asking her what she's into, and be prepared for a long discussion—or even argument. Just keep it friendly. When it seems like the conversation is coming to a conclusion, drop a hint about where you'll be later if she wants to pick up the thread.

Never, ever talk down to a girl or accuse her of "faking" geekiness to get attention from guys. If she's put down the cash for a con (and a costume), she's legit. Don't ruin your chances by insisting on some kind of pedigree. Plenty of (cute!) girls love the same geeky stuff as you, but they don't love getting harassed about it.

SEARCH OPTIMIZATION, PART 2: WHERE TO MEET NON-GEEKS

As I said earlier, limiting your love quest to the online world narrows your potential dating pool. So does restricting your search to geeks only. Sure, it's natural to want to find someone who shares your interests. But take it from me, there are plenty of intelligent, funny, perfectly lovely women out there who never learned that there is no spoon or that all your base are belong to us. Should they be denied access to your awesomeness because of that, Player One? I say thee nay!

If you're willing to cut the non-geek gals of world a break, here are some helpful strategies to turn a chance encounter into a close encounter.

The Non-Geek Social Gathering: Remember how I mentioned that expanding your social network, especially by adding more casual friendships, is a smart move? Here's a scenario where it can pay off big time. Meeting potential dates at a social gathering is one of the easiest ways to connect with somebody new. In most cases, you'll be with a mix of people, some you're already comfortable with and some you haven't met before. If someone new catches your eye, you have every excuse to say hi and strike up a conversation. Best of all, you can try to learn a bit about her before making an approach. Here's what to do:

Ask around. When you spot someone you'd like to meet, ask the host if he knows her. Check with other friends too. Keep the questions casual—you don't want to seem like a stalker—and definitely no drawings of "a girl with hair like this," Scott Pilgrim.

 Subtly work in the fact that you don't know the girl in question, and you might score a free introduction from your mutual friend.

YES	NO
"Hey, is that girl in the green dress a friend of yours? I don't think I've met her before."	"Dude, Green Dress Girl is hot. Does she have a boyfriend?"

Plant a flag. Social gatherings are tricky because the other people aren't browsing for books or games or anything that gives you instant insight to their personality. On the plus side, trivial break-the-ice-type chatter is expected, so it almost doesn't matter what you say, as long as it isn't obnoxious. If your host doesn't introduce you to the girl, approach her on your own and make a brief observation, compliment her, or make a joke.

YES	NO
"Awesome music—like dubstep meets Daft Punk." "Cool bracelet."	"Wow, you've got the most amazing eyes! Are they hazel or . . . no, they're kind of brown, aren't they? Quite beautiful."

Move on. After you've made your point, leave her to mull it over—like the Terminator, you'll be back, and you're giving yourself an instant conversation starter for when you return. Chat with your friends, grab a fresh drink, and *then* circle back. Recall your earlier comment (or let her do it for you!) and watch a conversation bloom. (Bonus: if she winced at the mention of dubstep but brightened at the mention of Daft Punk, you know she's got good musical taste.)

Join forces. If you're in luck (and the party doesn't totally suck), there'll be a cool activity you can invite her to do with you (karaoke, anyone?). But even something as basic as tracking down the snacks or refilling drinks can be a way to continue a conversation. By keeping things moving, you'll avoid making her feel like she's missing out on the party by spending too much time in one place.

Buddy up with your married-dude friends so you'll be invited to gatherings where you'll meet new women—when a guy gets hitched (or enters into a committed relationship with a woman), his social network expands to include all her female friends.

The bar: There's a sleazy stigma associated with meeting people in bars, which could make you wary of this scenario. But you might end up at some tavern or pub for all sorts of reasons: birthday parties, company happy hours, networking events, and live performances will all attract like-minded, potentially interesting individuals. Even if you're just out for a night of drinking with your dudes, there's no reason *not* to approach a girl if she looks like your type. Let's be honest—that's what bars are for. Here's the low-down:

Watch for the signs. Women often go to bars in groups (men do this too, of course). If you're wondering whether to approach a woman who's with her friends, observe the group dynamic. If they're huddled together and laughing, they're probably just there to have fun and not looking to meet anyone. But she's looking around the room while hanging with her crew, cancel red alert and make your move.

Straighten up and fly right. Her initial judgment of you will have much more to do with your posture and body language than anything you say. So no slouching. Stand tall and walk confidently. When you talk to her, maintain eye contact.

Start simply. Unlike almost every other location thus far, the bar has the unique advantage of being a recognized and time-tested place for picking people up. So even if she's not interested, you don't have to worry about being out of line just for trying. For high-traffic watering holes, turnaround can be fast, so don't waste time psyching yourself up. See a cute girl, say something (start with "hi"), and roll with it.

Watch her body language. If she smiles and maintains eye contact, that's a good sign. Other positive indicators: she does a quick "grooming audit" by touching her hair or clothes; she leans towards you; she mirrors some of your own body language or gestures. If she looks away, doesn't change her expression, replies in flat monosyllables, or unsnaps the catch on her holstered blaster, give it one more try, but then don't persist.

Ask questions. Ask her about herself, her job, how her day went, how she likes the cantina music in the background. Keep the chatting casual and your body language engaged: think leaning in or angling yourself towards her, not staring her down. You don't want her to feel like she's caught in the crosshairs.

Resist the urge to "neg" a girl, that is, say something slightly disparaging about her so she'll think you're not interested and lower her guard. Online pickup artists might tell you this gimmick works like a charm, but guess what—girls also read the Internet, they're onto the trick, and they hate it. Nix the neg.

 Buying a drink is a nice, even chivalrous gesture, but can do you more harm than good. A perfectly nice girl might be put off if she thinks you're doing it because you just want her to put out. Or worse, she'll take the drink and split without even learning your name.

The coffee shop: A large selection of beverages that will keep you up all night? Free Wi-Fi? Foods that are bad for you despite their fancy-sounding names (yeah, we're onto you, biscotti)? Of *course* coffee shops are an addictive place to hang out. Besides, ladies love a man who knows his lattés. Here's how to sweeten the pot:

Take your time taking it in. Bring a book or your laptop, settle in, and look around. Coffee shops can be quiet places, so there's no rush to make a scene with someone you're interested in. If you do see a promising candidate, glance at her over your laptop and see what she's drinking or reading—but don't linger too long, or you're risking creeperdom.

Make eyes. A coffee shop is a perfect place to practice wordless communication. Making a little eye contact, smile, and then looking away will show her you're interested and give her a moment to react while out of your gaze.

Get the go-ahead . . . Look back after a few moments. If she's smiling or returning your glance in a friendly manner, then you're good to go. If not, well, better luck next time.

. . . then go ahead. As you get up (to throw out trash, leave, or re-up on your espresso) stop by her table and comment on what she's doing, reading, or even drinking. Be complimentary, but don't lavish praise on her. A quick observation will do the trick.

YES	NO
"*A Song of Ice and Fire* is awesome. Do you watch the TV show, too?"	"What is that, a salted caramel macchiato? You look like you've got excellent taste, if you know what I mean [obnoxious wink]."
"*Advanced Classical Mechanics?* Are you a physics student?"	

The college classroom: Sure, you're in college for an education, but who says socialization isn't education? If you find your attention lingering on the lady in the front row of lecture instead of your professor's Powerpoint presentations, never fear. College classes are great places to meet someone, because you and she automatically have something in common.

Get close. Whether it's a six-person seminar or a cattle-call 101 course, you're never going to talk to her if she's too far away. Pick a seat around near hers, but leave a little personal space between.

Ask for help . . . If there's an aspect of the lecture that sailed right over your head, you've got yourself a conversation starter. But there's no need to play dumb here—just ask if you can borrow her notes from a class you missed, or check with her to see that you have the reading assignment right. It's a no-pressure way to start a conversation.

. . . or ask her opinion. See what she thought of the reading, or whether she *also* gets annoyed that your prof insists on formatting all his exams in Comic Sans. You can even get a friendly argument going over the class material—just be diplomatic. You're both academics, after all!

When conducting your conversations, keep the *extra* in *extracurricular*—don't talk during class. Otherwise, you risk pissing off your intended girl (or worse, your professor).

 If exams are looming, see if she wants to meet for a study session. It doesn't have to be one-on-one, either: even a group session will get you some more face time with her.

Should you feel truly bold, ask what she's got planned for the weekend. If she mentions a hobby or campus club, ask her about it. If she mentions that she'll be at a certain party, take the hint and go there.

More Ways to Meet Her IRL

Here are some other promising opportunities for meeting gals. In any of the following locales, remember to follow this basic walkthrough: Observe her briefly to assess her interests; say hi while making friendly, non-creepazoid eye contact; ask a question relevant to what she's doing; watch for positive body language; continue the conversation if things go well; move on politely if they don't.

Do volunteer work: Many women place a premium on selflessness in men. Just be certain you're there to do actual, helpful work as well as meet people.

Browse at a computer store: Is there a better place to find a gadget-loving geek gal?

Check out a new museum exhibit: Some surveys show that women are more impressed by intelligence and education than by looks.

Visit flea markets and antiques stores: There are plenty of unusual tchotchkes and gewgaws to talk about, and who knows—you might stumble across *Detective Comics #27* (a guy can dream, right?).

Boldly go anywhere else: Whether you're grocery shopping, hanging at the park, washing socks at the laundromat, or taking a pottery class at the community college, you're way more likely to meet people than if you're parked on your couch clicking through reruns on Hulu.

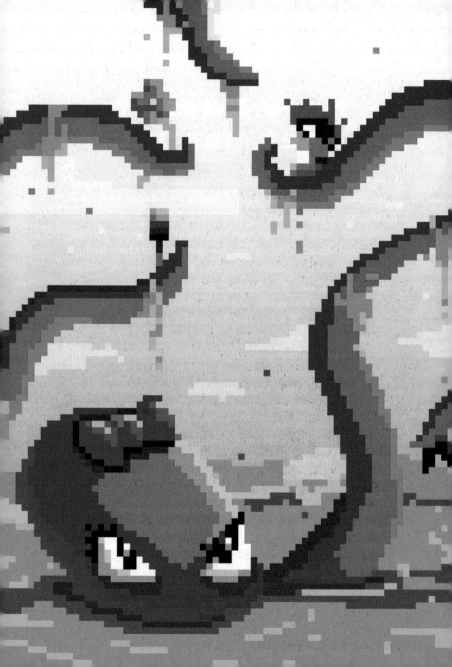

CHAPTER 3

Do or Do Not, There Is No Try: Asking Her Out

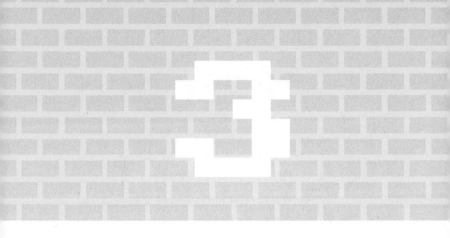

 o far, we've been approaching the dating process as though you're Solid Snake slowly advancing in an espionage mission, *Metal Gear Solid* style; ducking for cover while observing, analyzing, surveying, and exploring without taking immediate action.

There's nothing wrong with a little stealth, Player One. It makes for some critically acclaimed video games and, in real life, it lets you investigate the dating realm without getting hurt.

But as any gamer will tell you, eventually you have to come out from behind that comfortable cover if you want to advance to the next level. You can't snuggle up against that wall, blend into the tall reeds with your camouflage, or hide in that cardboard box forever. You've got to move ahead like Snake, knowing there is a chance you might get hurt. Life isn't a cut scene, and you don't earn points by hiding from what you're afraid of. You're Solid Snake, damn it. When things get tough you get up, clean yourself off, and continue forward.

Now is the time—to jump out of cover, to ditch the cardboard box, to hit B and skip the cut scene. It's time to man up and get out there. It's time to set up a date.

Preflight Checklist

As in any good stealth game, there are few important things to consider before you make your move—otherwise, you might just dash out of cover into the line of fire and wipe out before you see any action. So here's how to prep for the mission:

1. **Read Archived Dialogue Trees:** Have you asked any NPCs about this situation, namely, your friends, and maybe even the friends of the girl in question if you happen to have some in common? It's always good to gauge her interest in you, or what—if anything—you two have in common. If you haven't done so yet, throw out some casual questions: Is she dating anyone? Do you seem like her type of dude? If you already have asked, review those conversations for any red flags (recent breakups, psycho exes, demonic possessions, etc.).

2. **Review Your Inventory:** Are you appropriately prepared for a date in the first place? Do you have enough gold in your coin purse and the appropriate armor for an upcoming date? This step might seem premature, but what if she puts you on the spot? If this girl is interested and wants to hang out, say, *now*, you'll want to be ready—so do your homework.

3. **Check Your Skill Level:** This is the last—but definitely not least—pre-date preparatory step. Having your funds in order and your outfits ready won't help you if you yourself aren't ready to do the actual asking. There's nothing wrong with a few training sessions first: plan what you want to say and then run it by a friend, or even practice a few lines in the mirror so you can deliver them smoothly when the time comes. It might feel weird, but it's helpful, and totally normal, too . . . unless you're Robert De Niro in *Taxi Driver*. Then there's some serious damage there that you need to address, stat.

Okay, so: you've reviewed past conversations, you've looked at your inventory, and you're confident that your skill level is high enough to push forward? Awesome! Make it so, (Player) Number One. Let's emerge from the swamp (but please, don't eat any snakes) and learn how to take that first big step.

Stage Select

When you're getting ready to ask someone out, your choices for venue lie before you like the levels of Mario Kart. Okay, maybe it's not the best metaphor, but you get the idea: different places offer different advantages (and disadvantages) for your performance. Be sure to pick the right one: just as you wouldn't start off full-speed on Rainbow Road, you shouldn't necessarily jump right to point-blank, in-person date requests before you're ready.

> ### KEY:
>
> **Difficulty Level:** How hard it will be to ask someone out using this specific tactic, on a scale of 1 (cakewalk) to 10 (sticking your hand in a nerve induction box while threatened by a gom jabbar).
>
> **Terrain:** A general sense of the lay of the land.
>
> **Track tips:** What to watch out for as you're cruisin' through.

TRACK: TELEPHONE TALKIN'

Difficulty Level: 5

Terrain: Asking someone out on the phone is a great beginner approach, no matter if you've known the person for a few minutes or a few years. Whether you met your dream geek and managed to get her phone number (WIN!) or things seem to be getting a little more than friendly with a friend you've known for a while, go ahead and dial her up. If you've got her number, chances are she's comfortable talking to you, so it'll be a smooth ride.

Track tips:

- **Take your time.** Jump right in and start a conversation, but don't feel the need to floor the accelerator to get things moving. The only thing worse than awkward silence is incoherent babbling. Breathe, Player One. Be casual, friendly, and relaxed.

- **Be prepared.** That awkward silence we just mentioned? Avoid it at all costs. Stock up on potential topics to cover before you cross the finish line (keep a crib sheet handy if you need to— phone contact puts you in visual stealth mode).

- **Try not to text.** I'm sure a lot of your friends have said it's okay to ask someone out via text message. But the character constraints of a text make it work like a racing game speed boost: the force of getting a lot across in not a lot of space can propel you forward so fast you end up spinning out. Look at it from her point of view: Reading a text? Short, but not always sweet. Hearing someone's voice? Much more sincere.

TRACK: SOCIAL MEDIA SCHMOOZIN'

Difficulty Level: 1–4

Terrain: Deceptively familiar, but not without its twists, turns, and occasional bumps. Forget the lurkers of old-school BBSes and IRC channels: this is the age of social media, and everyone's online now. Asking a girl for her Twitter handle, or looking her up on Facebook, is perfectly normal these days. But the approach isn't always straightforward. Pick an appropriate route, keep your eyes open, and be ready to pull a 180 in case of crisis.

On Facebook, if you remember her name and have mutual friends, you've got a direct path to follow. Twitter, on the other hand, isn't a fantastic place for meeting your potential love interest. Much more exposed and with no safety barriers, the public platform is better for networking with people in your field, finding drink specials, and getting story leads.

Track tips for Facebook:

- **Read her profile.** Facebook pages are like a personal map. Is she seeing someone? How often does she update? Does she even seem like someone you'd date in the first place? Keep an eye out for traps: "In a relationship" is an obvious red flag, but her "likes" can tell you a lot too.
- **Think before friending.** Everyone has their own protocol regarding their social media profiles, so it's important to tread carefully on these virtual grounds. Not everyone adds every single stranger they meet as their Facebook friend, or even every casual acquaintance. Does she have a ton of friends? That's a green light—she's probably fairly open with her Facebook account, so you shouldn't be afraid of sending her that surprise friend request. An average amount of friends, say a few hundred? Yellow: proceed with caution. Fewer than fifty? Hit the brakes.
- **Chat conservatively.** That little green dot is lit up, but think twice before starting your engine. If she's busy seeing what friends are up to online, browsing through vacation pictures, or updating her job history, she might not want to be disturbed (not everyone

on chat remembers to go invisible). Besides, the more time you spend swapping instant messages back and forth on Facebook, the less reason she has see you in person. Be bold, hit the accelerator, and ask her to hang out as soon as possible.

Track tips for Twitter:

- **Watch for mirages.** Forget about how "easy" it is to "connect" with people on Twitter. That's an illusion. You're not really learning about the person behind the account. Who is she, outside of this online persona? What does she care about? What does she *actually* look like? Try to verify these details with a reliable source before making any moves.
- **Be comfortable out in the open.** If you @ somebody, you're sending your message in front of everyone. Imagine standing up in a crowded room, screaming across the room and asking someone you really don't know out on a date. Imagine she says no, in front of absolutely everyone. You *can* have a private conversation on there, using Direct Messaging, but you can't direct message someone on Twitter unless she also follows you. And if she is, she's probably your friend IRL, in which case . . .
- **Don't ask out an IRL friend.** If you're actually friends—or even acquaintances—you really shouldn't ask her out with an @. It's rude and weird. Unless this is some kind of cute inside joke between the two of you, steer clear.

TRACK: IN-PERSON PARLEY

Difficulty Level: 8–10 (aka "Boss Level")

Terrain: Straightforward and smooth, the in-person approach is built for speed. It can be the most difficult, but, at the same time, the most effective way to ask someone out. It shows that you're direct, you take charge, and you're confident. Plus, in this age of texts and tweets, she may be impressed that you've got the gumption and integrity to ask her out face-to-face. That said, with less room for error, you'll want to double-check your prep work: don't just gauge her interest and ensure that you have things in common, but also survey the road ahead with these tips. Because hey, you're rolling Boss Level now, and this is how we do, aight?

Track Tips:

- **Sync your schedule.** You're about to ask someone out. In person. So before you put yourself on the spot, make sure you're prepared. In the event of a yes, you don't want to stand there, awkwardly fidgeting with your calendar on your smartphone as you discover you're not free for another two weeks. Don't make yourself seem like you're unreliable or unavailable before the first date; have a plan in mind before opening your mouth.

- **Polish your appearance.** You're IRL now, and you want to look your best when you're making your move (check Chapter 4 for more tips on suiting up).

- **Speak body language.** Keep it open and cool—no crossed arms, fidgeting hands, or shifty eyes. "Echoing" someone's body postures can help them relax and open up around you.

- **Be clear about your intent.** Don't leave her wondering what you mean by "hanging out" or "doing something some time." If you do your job right, she should have no doubt that you want to take her out and show her a good time.

- **Stay on track.** Stick with specifics. Focus. Don't let yourself get distracted and drift away from the dating stuff.

- **Don't floor it.** Just like on the phone, be cool when making that specific suggestion—don't rush. There's nothing to be nervous about (really!), and stammering through "ums" and "ers" will see you run out of steam long before the finish line.

Go, Speed Dater, Go!

Speed dating, an organized event in which singles meet each other in fast succession, isn't dating as such. Typically, you have to register and pay a fee to participate, and then you'll get a 3- to 5-minute chat with each female participant. When it's all over, you decide who you'd like to follow up with . . . but you only get her contact info if she also wants to date you.

In short, speed dating is an opportunity to meet strangers who will judge, in a matter of minutes, whether or they want to date you. Is this rapid-fire approach worth a shot? To decide, let's compare it to *Speed Racer*. Because you may not have been speed dating, but I bet you've seen at least one episode of the Japanese animated television series from the 1960s (for our purposes, that Wachowski movie version never happened).

Speed dating and *Speed Racer* have one crucial, essential thing in common: speed. No, seriously. In *Speed Racer*, cut-rate animation techniques—recycling backgrounds, reusing action sequences, and redrawing only the mouths in Speed's or Trixie's close-ups to make them talk—saved precious man hours. Speed dating also takes a lot of shortcuts, cramming ten or more introductions into a single evening and forcing you to speak as quickly as the voice actors who dubbed for Speed, Pops, and Spritle. You'll definitely meet a variety of new people, but you'll probably end up repeating some of the same dialogue over and over. (You: "I just started this cool job. It doesn't pay a lot but I really enjoy it." Speed: *"Ohhhhhhhhhh!"*)

Is speed good for dating? Studies do show that we can make up our minds about people very quickly, even as fast as three seconds. But there's also research showing that in speed dating, women focus on superficialities like appearance more than deeper traits like intelligence. If you're prepared to gun the car around the track for several laps of rat-a-tat meet-and-greets, search online for a local speed date event that isn't too costly and is held in an appropriate venue (restaurant, bar, and student union are okay; somebody's garage, nuh-uh). Be sure to spruce up, since good grooming and body language will likely win out over sloppy charm and wit. Adventure's waiting just ahead. Be friendly and positive, and please, please, don't bring your kid brother or his pet chimp.

To Boldly Go . . . Where?

As I've said, Player One, before you ask her out, it's a good idea to have a destination in mind. True, it's unlikely you and your new companion will immediately hop into a TARDIS and head off to dinner on Gallifrey (before it was destroyed). But you don't want to get stuck faltering at the other end of the "what did you have in mind?" question. Consider some of these surefire first date destinations:

- **Museums:** Show that you're cultured and intelligent. Big, open spaces like art museums give you the opportunity to walk around in a beautiful setting while getting to know each other. And some of them (see below) can be quiet and intimate.

 If you're one of those people who doesn't "get" art, try a science museum, a transit museum, etc. Chances are there's a small, quirky, niche cultural attraction somewhere in your area that you can explore together.

- **Restaurants:** There's no reason you should feel like you have to go to some incredible five-star restaurant on a first date: your favorite local gastropub is just fine (if you don't have one, scour the Internet for recommendations). Choose a place that's relatively relaxed—you'll want to be able to hear each other—and scout it in advance if you can.

 Clear your restaurant choice with your date before making the reservation—you don't want to bring her to Dave's Finest Dead Animal BBQ only to find out that she's a lifelong vegetarian.

- **Long walks:** Plan a nice relaxed stroll through the city or a local park and get to know each other. Take in the nice weather and enjoy the day together. Bring along a picnic if you think you'll get hungry. This is a great option if you feel the need to keep things informal at first. But don't take long walks in the winter. This isn't *Game of Thrones*.

 Enhance your jaunt, and make it more datelike, with a visit to an outdoor festival, flea market, or farm stand.

- **Used books or music store:** These joints provide plenty of opportunity to get to know a person. Old records, used paperbacks, discounted CDs, and quarter-bin comic books are all instant conversation fodder to get you chatting about shared musical interests, authors you like or dislike, etc. Choose a place with a coffee shop or restaurant nearby so you can keep things going afterwards.

- **Video games:** A video game date is totally an acceptable date—as long as this potential love interest *likes video games*. Take her to an arcade, or choose a fun game you can play together at home while talking. Remember that this should be a shared activity: don't play the latest single-player RPG while she watches you jerk your joystick.

- **Outdoor adventures:** If you're both nature-loving types, a hike, bike ride, or trip to jump in a lake can make for a perfect date. In colder months, you can try something as adventurous as cross-country skiing or as low-tech as a snowball fight.

 Danger and romantic attraction don't only intertwine in Indiana Jones movies: research shows that sharing something that gets the ol' adrenaline pumping increases the likelihood that there will be a spark between you and your date.

While a number of your favorite hangouts might seem like excellent venues for this encounter, you'd be surprised at how many are actually danger zones for getting to know someone. Think twice before heading to:

- **The movies:** Hear me out on this one. Yes, a movie is a classic, almost obvious, location for a date. And, as a geek, there is always something playing on the silver screen you're passionate about. But the whole purpose of a first date is to get to know someone, and that's kind of hard to accomplish when you're sitting in silence through a two-hour Jackie Chan flick. (Exception: Lots of cities offer free outdoor movie screenings in the summertime, so take advantage and take a date—you'll be able to talk to her and bring way better snacks than stale popcorn drowned in that fake-butter stuff.)

- **Concerts:** This is another risky choice for a first date. Blaring music and sticky floors aren't exactly romantic. Play it safe and save this setting for a future date.

- **Clubs:** The music is loud, you're surrounded by people who are on the prowl, you'll have to yell to talk to each other, and it's impossible to get a drink refill . . . not a good idea.

- **Events with friends or family:** Not only is it a little weird to introduce a date to your friends or family this early on, you're losing prime get-to-know-her time. You'll spend more time introducing your relatives and listening to other people ask her questions than you will talking to her one-on-one. Plus, let's face it, dude, your brother is *weird*.

Red Five Standing By: How to Deploy Your Wingman

Finding it necessary to party up to complete your quest? Don't feel bad. The geek canon is full of legendary wingmen who helped their partners level up, and for good reason: whether you're dogfighting with MiGs, trench-diving in your X-wing, or making a controlled approach towards an attractive redhead, wingmen rock.

So review your friend list for potential wingmen, Player One, because when it's time for your attack run, you need Wedge Antilles, not Biggs Darklighter. Look for these stats, and while you're at it, brush up on them yourself—the best way to recruit a great wingman is to be willing to return the favor.

POSITIVE WINGMAN ATTRIBUTES

In a Relationship
Bonus Stats: -100 Threat Level, +50 to Appearance

A wingman in a serious relationship (i.e., he has a girlfriend or is engaged or married) shows that you hang out with guys who are trustworthy and commitment-prone. Plus, you won't have to worry about him moving in on your territory, and, as mentioned last chapter, he's your connection to his wife's single friends. (This is the one guy you don't want to be a wingman *for*, so you'll have to find another way to pay him back. Maybe babysit?)

More Extroverted than You
Bonus Stats: +150 to Speech

An ideal wingman is outgoing, talkative, and immediately easy to get along with. He'll be there to help plug lulls in conversation and, if necessary, get you chatting as well.

Common Ground
Bonus Stats: +25 All Character Attributes
Be sure that your wingman shares some kind of solid, common ground with you. The two of you should have a history together, a similar sense of humor, and the ability to play off each other's jokes, quips, and stories—all of which helps you stay relaxed and comfortable. Combine this with the previous trait for a killer combo.

Has Your Back
Bonus Stats: +100 to Defense
So you're talking to your dream geekette. Chances are, if you're at a convention or a party, a lot of other NPCs have noticed her too, and will circle back like vultures after they finish rummaging through the $1 comic bins or wrapping up that game of *Mario Party*. A great wingman will carry with him his Epic Shield of Blocking and prevent those moochers from interrupting your conversation with the lady.

Epic Loot/Bag of Holding

Bonus Stats: +500 Gold, +25 to Defense

If you're out at a bar or a restaurant, a wingman has your back when the Mana Potions run dry. He is ready, willing, and able to run out and grab you and that possible future significant other a beverage when you're tapped—allowing you to maintain contact with the gal and keep the conversation going. A good wingman also carries other useful items you might forget: a smartphone, pen and paper (so you can jot down your number), coins for the parking meter, breath-freshening gum or mints.

Sharp Eye for Style

Bonus Stats: +250 to Armor

A quality wingman's work doesn't start at an event or when you're out on the town. It begins earlier, when you're out shopping or getting ready to hit the street. He should know enough about basic grooming and current men's fashion to give you honest feedback about your appearance, letting you know if you look less like Tony Stark and a little more like The Thing.

NEGATIVE WINGMAN ATTRIBUTES

Better Looking than You

Bonus Stats: -250 to Your Physical Appearance

Through no fault of his (or your) own, a significantly better-looking wingman might pull interest away from you, or even make you look downright crummy in comparison. I know you're not into evaluating the attractiveness of dudes, Player One, but try to choose wingman whose looks are on par with your own.

Has No Idea He's the Wingman

Bonus Stats: -100 to All Character Attributes

Don't take chances: make sure your wingman *knows* he is playing this role, Player One. He could be the most extroverted, loot-dropping-est wingman in the history of wingmen, but without the knowledge that he is there to help *you* out, chances are he will be off on his own quest. Make sure he is properly recruited to your party before starting off, and don't neglect to return the favor if he asks.

Member of the Opposite Sex

Bonus Stats: 50% chance +100 Suspicion, 50% chance +100 Trust

This is a tricky one. A wingman of the opposite sex (wingwoman?) can be amazing or terrible. In some cases she can definitely help out by picking up on signals you might otherwise miss. In other cases, her presence might make other women suspicious—and they have every right to be. Who is this woman? Why are the two of you so close? What's your history together? If you do go the girl-power route, have a friendly chat with your winglady-to-be before taking flight, so she'll know when to ease up on the throttle and give you some room to maneuver.

Release the Kraken! How to Ask Her Out

When asking someone out, some of us choke. (And guess what? So do non-geeks.) We do the verbal equivalent of button mashing: say whatever pops into our head, moving from thought to speech with no real strategy.

I'll help you break down this important invitation into key moves and use them effectively. Because whether you're asking out a girl or playing Super Smash Brothers, the right combos will get the right results.

THE CONTROLS

Familiarize yourself with these key moves. Practice them. Recast them in your own words until you can access them at will.

X = Warmup Question
"How are you?"
"What's up?"
"How's it going?"

□ = Ask about Schedule
"What are you doing tonight?"
"Do you have any plans on [day of week]?"

O = Mention Activity
"There's this cool [date idea] coming up."
"I've been meaning to check out [date idea]."

△ = Pull the Trigger
"Do you want to go out?"

★ = Compliment
"You're a lot of fun to hang out with."
"I think you're cute."

→ = Advance
"It'll be a lot of fun."
"The weather's going to be great."
"I've heard [date idea] is awesome."

← = Retreat
"Just thought I'd put it out there."
"Only if it sounds like fun."
"No pressure."
"Figured it was worth a shot."

THE COMBOS

Once you have the basic moves down, you can mix and match them to fit the situation, jumping and dodging and blocking and shooting until it's victory or game over. Start with these suggested combinations, but feel free to craft your own signature maneuvers.

The Take-Your-Time: X + □ + ○ + △
A good move for easing into the big question.

The Direct Approach: ★ + △
Maximum effect with minimal effort.

The Jump-Off Point: □ + ○ + △
Good for when you need to look before you leap.

The Shoot-First-Details-Later: △ + ○
Fire away for immediate results.

The Stealth: ○ + ➔ + ★ + △
Good for avoiding detection.

The Two-Step: X + △ , then ← + ★
Forth and back for a quick recovery.

The Hard Sell: ○ + ➔ + △
Bring down defenses with an awesome activity.

THE FINISHING MOVE

So, you did it. Victory. Round over. Hopefully, she said yes. (She didn't? You're a better man for asking. See "If She Says No," opposite.)

No matter your combo of choice, the end of your question means the beginning of the game. But this means you've got to make plans . . . logistical plans. You'll probably be glowing (not literally) with the gleam of conquest, but don't get caught up in your emotions and dash away without knowing the details: when you're going to meet, who will call whom, and how you both will get to where you're going. Once that's established, make a graceful retreat. You've got preparations to make.

If She Says No: How Epic Fails Make You a Better Player

Whether the game is Minesweeper, Megaman, or an MMO, failure can really blow up in your face (literally, in the case of Minesweeper). Dating's no different. Even when you employ your best strategy, sometimes you get shot down anyway. And in both instances, it's hard not to feel like . . . well, a loser.

Take heart, Player One. In the long run, rejections are totally for the win. Not to sound like the dad from *Calvin and Hobbes*, but if a girl brushes you off, calls you out, or just politely rejects you, you're building character. Each crash and burn is another few points in your XP bar, bringing you closer to leveling up. Look at this way:

You're learning what doesn't work. So maybe you're staring a little too hard at a girl before making your move. Maybe you're mumbling and not making yourself heard the first time. Maybe you shouldn't have started that Star Wars vs. Star Trek smackdown with the cute Vulcan cosplayer. S'all good: now you know what not to do.

You're grinding your dating ability. Just like an RPG requires you to spend endless hours gathering and crafting to up your skill in a particular discipline, dating requires an investment of time as well. Before you can blacksmith up an epic broadsword, you're gonna crank out a lot of dinky rings and helms. Hey, they can't all be awesome!

You're making good use of your armor. You don't clothe your RPG character in the best plate armor possible just so he can strut around and look awesome (okay, maybe that's part of it). You employ that stuff because it's made to get beaten up, and there's no point to wearing it if you never put yourself into the fray. And unlike plate mail, your emotional hide actually thickens when it gets clobbered by a rejection, so after some healing time you can jump back into the fracas. Besides, the only thing worse than a girl saying she's not interested is a girl saying nothing at all—because she doesn't even know you exist.

Escape from the Friendzone

Have you heard any (or all) of these following statements over the course of your pursuit?

> "I don't want to complicate our friendship."
> "You're like, I don't know, a brother to me."
> "I have so much fun with you!"
> "[Insert lengthy discussions about problems with other love interests here]" followed by "so what do you think I should do?" or "I feel like I can talk to you about anything."
> "I just met someone amazing!"
> "Sure! I'd love to go out with you tonight! I'll invite all my friends."

If so, you probably feel like you're stuck in an alternate reality. A twilight realm where you're considered a close, valuable, worthwhile companion—but not boyfriend material. You, Player One, are trapped in the Friendzone.

Much like the wraithlike denizens of the Phantom Zone, you might feel stuck in time in the Friendzone, unable to make your love interest see or hear your true romantic intentions. But unlike the Phantom Zone, your time in the Friendzone can actually become something quite valuable, and a lot less hellish-interdimensional-limbo-like. Here are some exit strategies.

The friendship route: If you're spending so much time with someone of the opposite sex, we already know you're a great person whom she likes having around. But as impressed as she is with your vast collections of video games and comics, your quick-witted television and movie references, something just isn't there. Guess what? You're still *friends*. There's something about you that she values unlike any other person, and that's significant. Get out of the Friendzone and accept your place in the pantheon of her true friends (and remember that a true friend doesn't hold a grudge for being rebuffed romantically).

The strike quickly route: Timing is everything, even if you're driving the time-traveling DeLorean from the *Back to the Future* franchise. The number one reason guys can't take things to the next level with a woman is because they've waited too long to make a move. So when you feel the Friendzone closing in you, act quickly, like Marty McFly charging up the flux capacitor during a thunderstorm. Hit the gas pedal and floor it to 88 mph while there's still a chance lightning will strike.

The I-know-kung-fu route: Having a close female friend lets you test some of your dating strategies without the fear of injuring yourself . . . kind of like the martial arts training that Neo underwent in *The Matrix*. Your female friend has a perspective you don't (i.e., that of a female). Ask her for help with your best lines and get invaluable insight. And who knows, hearing about your romantic yearnings may help her see you as the desirable catch you are.

The Philip J. Fry route: For the first several seasons of *Futurama*, Fry is a textbook dweller of the Friendzone. Leela, his one-eyed, purple-haired mutant coworker whom he adores so completely (hey, the heart wants what it wants) has zero interest in him. Nevertheless, over time we slowly witness Fry capture Leela's heart. How does he do it? For one thing, he knows not to push the issue (usually). Leela knows how he feels, and she only has to karate-kick him back to reality every few episodes. It's not Fry's frequent, usually misguided, schemes to win her over that eventually do the trick, though. It's his sincerity. Every time Fry has an amazing, almost unfair advantage that would seal the deal with Leela (increased intellect and strength due to space parasites; robotic hands that make him the galaxy's greatest musician), he gives it up in favor of building a sincere relationship. And in the end, he gets that kiss.

Go and do likewise, Player One. Selflessness and nobility may be a difficult path to follow. But if it leads you out of the Friendzone, the kiss will be all the sweeter.

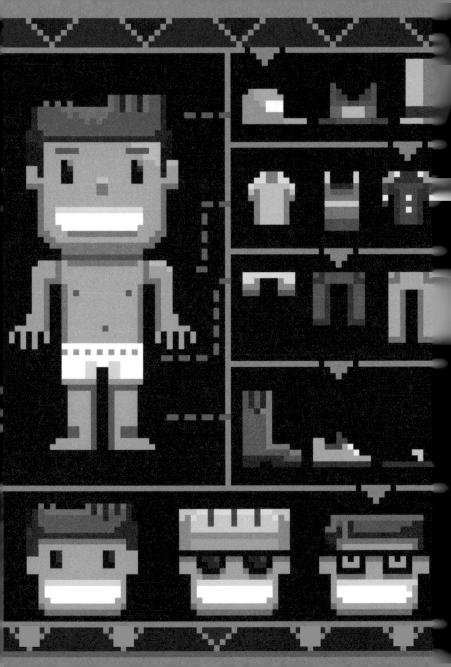

CHAPTER 4

Ready, Player One? Preparing for the Date

ating is supposed to be fun, but that doesn't mean it's always easy. After all, you're putting yourself out there, exposed, prepared for what might very well be rejection or eventual heartbreak (but hopefully will be acceptance and mutual enjoyment). Like a superhero, you're trying to use your powers and abilities to make the world a better place (your world, at least). But unlike comic book heroes everywhere, you're out there without a secret identity to protect you.

It's no wonder you may be feeling daunted, Player One. And if you've been knocked out of the sky before, it can be especially hard to slip the cape back on and jump into the fray. But just as almost every great superhero or heroine has at one point been defeated—even killed*—you can resurrect yourself even after a seemingly fatal blow.

In this chapter, we'll explore ways to get yourself physically and emotionally ready to date—no masks needed.

---

*Superman, Professor X, Elektra, Hawkeye, The Thing, Jean Grey, Deadpool, Spawn, Green Lantern, Green Arrow, The Flash, Flaming Carrot . . . the list goes on and on.

The Kolinahr: Check Your Emotional Baggage

If it's been a while since you dated or your recent dates haven't been particularly successful, it doesn't hurt to take a quick emotional inventory before your next round. If you happen to be a Vulcan, this effort might culminate in a years-long sabbatical to purge all your emotions and achieve pure logic. But for us humans, this version of the Kolinahr is much less extreme; you simply want to become more aware of any fear, cynicism, or jadedness you might have about dating. Characters in tabletop RPGs used to have a carrying capacity limited by their strength (and routinely ignored by players determined to grab every last copper piece in the dungeon). You, meanwhile, have an *emotional* carrying capacity, and ignoring that could leave your psyche so burdened with emotional baggage that you can't move forward in dating. Here are some items to consider jettisoning from your inventory (or at least putting into storage for now).

Hearthstone. If you're a chronic homebody, you might feel a bit of extra anxiety when dating puts you in an unfamiliar environment. Make a point of getting out of the house more often than usual, so you'll be more at ease on your date even without a magic rock to teleport you home. It can also help to visit the locale of your upcoming rendezvous in advance, so you'll know the lay of the land.

Armor. We all have our own defenses, but if you're not a dwarven berserker or Captain America, there's no reason to carry a shield everywhere you go. And it's hard for someone to get to know you if your face is hidden by a medieval helm. Don't let defensiveness become your primary character trait. Leave the chain mail at home, and try enjoy whatever sparring takes place during your date.

Hi-def vision. Whether it's the microscopic vision of a Kryptonian or the thermal goggles of the *Metal Gear* series, superhuman eyesight can be a big advantage. But when you're on a date, Player One, it doesn't pay to examine her every move under an electron microscope. While you're scanning for some hidden signal or deeper meaning, you'll miss out on what's happening right in front of your eyes.

Ammunition. You've probably got some idea already of what works for you when talking to women, and I'm hoping you're finding lots of new ideas in this book. But don't treat your growing stockpile of compliments and conversation topics like so many rounds of ammunition to fire in rapid succession until you hit a target. You're a guy, not some kind of weird proclamation-spewing date robot. You have to engage her in spontaneous, *two-way* interactions, in which you hear what she's saying and respond accordingly. Bring ideas, stories, and questions to the table, not fact-blasts and bullet-pointed lists.

 Keep your own emotional baggage properly stowed. But don't be tempted to start a relationship based on the idea that you can sort out someone else's issues. She won't appreciate being treated like a project, and you won't be able to form a genuine connection with her.

The Pon Farr: Physical Preparation

You may have a great personality and winning smile. You may even have saved the universe dozens of times from horrifying superbeings from beyond the cosmos. Maybe you're honorable and just, bound by a code of honor. But if you show up on your first date wearing nothing but a tattered trench coat with an awful beard, sorry. That first date is going nowhere.

First impressions matter, as unfair as that sometimes may be. When the Thing started courting blind sculptress Alicia Masters, he dressed up properly, even though he was an idol of millions and she couldn't see that he was basically made of orange rock. Choosing what you're going to wear and making sure you're properly groomed are, in fact, pretty damn important—not because you want to appear as something you're not, but because it shows you consider her well worth the effort. If you're a Vulcan, whose Pon Farr mating frenzy dictates they only date once every seven years or so, you have plenty of time to prepare. The rest of you, keep reading.

BUILDING A BULLETPROOF WARDROBE

Just as in any RPG, your clothes are more than just a way to keep you from being naked—they communicate to the world who you are. We geeks know this, of course (hmmm . . . should I wear my House of Targaryen shirt to tonight's gaming session, or my C:\ DOS\RUN tee?). But selecting your wardrobe for a date is less about establishing geek cred than about proving yourself as someone she can see herself hanging out with in public. I'd never tell you to get rid of your replica Imperial officer's cap, Player One. I'm just advising you to invest in some quality, grown-up clothes too.

If your closet's bare, don't despair—putting a decent wardrobe together is easier than it sounds. As a guy, your armor has really just two modes, depending on where you're planning to stage your battle: Casual and Dressy. Let's break them down:

Casual Mode. There's a huge difference between date casual and playing-video-games-or-D-&-D-with-the-guys-in-my-apartment-all-day casual. Cutoff sweatpants are *never* date casual.

YES: Dark jeans or khakis. Make sure these fit you at the waist and that they're not too short or too long. The cuffs should reach hit your shoes with a single, slight crease (or "break") at the ankle—more than one break means they're too long, and if your socks are showing, they're too short. Shop for a straight leg or slim cut rather than boot cut. If you can't find a perfect fit in the store, many tailors will work with jeans to get them just right.

NO: Sweatpants. Shorts, too (although they *might* be acceptable if you've planned an outdoor activity; if you're uncertain, forget it).

YES: A simple, solid-colored, *logo-free* T-shirt or a short-sleeved dress shirt—aka a collared shirt of some kind (polo or button-down style). Make sure it fits; larger-sized shirts may be comfy, but you look better when you're not drowning in fabric. You want a good fit across your shoulders—no straining or sagging.

Research has shown that ladies love a man in red—the color evokes desirable attributes like power, heat, and (ahem) virility.

NO: T-shirts with goofy sayings, pop culture references, or inside jokes. While I'm all for letting your geek flag fly, a "geeky" shirt actually works against you in this regard—it literally labels you and makes you seem like one-dimensional, which we all know you're not. (Remember *Shrek*? Your personality's got layers, dude.) Band T-shirts are a possible exception if the design is arty enough (or the band is awesome enough). Just don't look like a billboard.

YES: Collared long-sleeved shirts and casual sweaters. Button-down collars are a more casual look; a sweater tends to make a fancy shirt seem less dressy. Flannel shirts are acceptable

- casual wear (you hipster, you) as long as they're in good shape.
- Stick with a classic crew or V-neck for sweaters, and remember, fit is everything.
- **NO:** Windbreakers, studded belts, or hoodies. Especially all at once.

Dressy Mode. Getting dressed up isn't all that big a deal, and you'll manage just fine when you've got the right things in your armory.

- **YES:** A light blazer or a sport jacket. As with shirts, fit is crucial here. Sleeves should reach your wrists and no further, shoulder seams should lie on your shoulder, and no weird divots or wrinkles should pop up. Try to shop where the clerks can advise you on fit and color. That said, very few fitted jackets will fit perfectly off the rack, so be prepared to get friendly with a local tailor—the Q to your Bond, if you will. Trust me: it's worth the extra step (and expense).
- **NO:** Anything dressier, like a tuxedo. Unless you happen to be catching a once-in-a lifetime staging of *Maria & Draco*, avoid overdressing.
- **YES:** Dark jeans (less dressy) or slacks (more). Jeans can be acceptable for the low end of dressing up, but make sure they fit (see above) and come in a dark wash (or black) with no weird fading or "artistic" rips. And of course they should be free of stains or rips. Slacks—aka "dress pants"—should fit close to the leg with no resistance or billowing. Aim for a single break above the ankle and no more.
- **NO:** Short sleeve shirt with a tie. This combo only works if you're managing a supermarket.
- **NO:** Anything noticeably odd. A smoking jacket? Seriously? That Holden Caulfield model deerstalker hat? Keep it in the closet, Holmes. A fedora? I hate to break it to you, but no one's

looked good in that hat since Sinatra. Save your idiosyncratic "trademark" wardrobe items for later dates, when she'll be more comfortable with your attempts at self-expression.

YES: Nice-looking accessories. A solid-color belt is always good as decoration (but if you need it to keep your pants up, they're too big. To the tailor's!). A money clip or an understated billfold is a classy way to carry cash. If you want to wear a tie, go for it: it should fall to just the top of your waistband and sit comfortably under (but not tighten) your collar. And again, keep the wacky, gimmicky ties in the drawer for now.

NO: Man jewelry. I don't care how epic your loot is, the last thing you want to do is wear more bling than your date does. Limit this to a wristwatch and maybe a single, not-too-flashy ring.

Shoes. If you're anything like me, you have a hard time selecting footwear, and would rather hit up the local Payless than visit a high-end shoe boutique. Don't be tempted to give up and go Frodo—no one wants to see your hobbit feet, dude. You don't need to drop a lot of gold to score some damn fine footwear. Just keep these tips in mind:

Sneakers: Keep them classic and simple—dark colors and laces, low cut, and no running shoes (save those for when you're actually running).

Casual shoes: You can't go wrong with classic leather loafers, bucks, or "boat shoes" (aka Top-Siders). Stay away from the clog-like sneaker/shoe hybrids (think Clarks and Merrells) unless you're going hiking.

Boots: Desert boots (leather and around ankle height) in a dark brown or tan are almost universally flattering, but anything that's leather with a leather sole is best. Avoid anything too decorated or studded—if it looks too weird for your grandpa to wear in the old days, it's probably not a classic look.

- **Dress shoes:** Spring for the nicest materials you can (genuine leather, with a sole that's stitched on and not glued) and you'll get your money's worth. Black really only works with black and gray, so opt for brown if you want versatility (generally, the lighter the brown, the more casual the look). Avoid square toes—go for a round or "chisel" shape.

    For a good fit, make sure that your toes barely graze the front of the shoe and that you can't easily fit a finger behind your heel. And they should be comfortable—don't think you can "break them in."

LOOT THIS LOOK: HOW TO EMULATE THE BEST-DRESSED GUYS IN THE GEEK CANON

You're looking at yourself in the mirror, admiring the threads you've decided to wear on your special evening: T-shirt with a built-in speaker that blasts a selection of hilarious music you've programmed, jeans held up by a belt with an LED buckle that spells out an assortment of witty pop-culture catchphrases, roguish fedora tipped over one eye . . .

Player One, *please* don't do this. If you want to go beyond the fashion basics I've laid out and upgrade to something more stylish, look no further than your geek heroes.

The Look: *The (New) Doctor (Doctor Who)*
Loot it by wearing: Dark-colored dress shirts, leather jackets, striped vests, blazers, subtle (read: non-obnoxious) bow ties, glasses

There's a reason why the Doctor's companions so often fall in love with him. And it isn't his uncanny ability to save their lives every other episode.

It's the bow ties.

Starting with the introduction of Christopher Eccleston as the

Doctor in 2005, the BBC's handsome time traveler with two hearts has become quite the stylish alien. Through his modern reincarnations since the show's revival, we've seen the Doctor dressed with a geek-chic look that, although carefully planned, makes him appear as if he isn't trying. There's lots going on with this look, so appropriate it one element at a time and get feedback from family and friends. As for the bow tie, it *must* be the real deal, no clip-ons. Find a YouTube video that shows how to tie it properly.

The Look: *Han Solo (Star Wars)*
Loot it by wearing: Black jeans or pants, light long-sleeved shirt, dark vest

Despite getting dressed in a galaxy far, far away, everyone's favorite space smuggler actually has a pretty good look for Earth dates. This combo is roguish but classy, won't attract unwanted attention in a cantina, and is simple enough to put together quickly when you need to outrun Imperial starships (not the local bulk cruisers, mind you). Don't worry about getting too buttoned up, but do keep your waistband tucked in if you're worried about looking sloppy. (Hokey religions or not, there's no need to keep a blaster at your side.)

The Look: *Neo (The Matrix)*
Loot it by wearing: Black trench coat, black T-shirt, black pants, black sunglasses…

No one disagrees that Neo has a totally bad-ass look, and with the right clothes, you too can be transformed from Mr. Anderson to the One. Not everyone can pull of the Man in Black look, though, so consider lightening things up by swapping in some gray or dark-colored items.

The Look: *Captain Mal Reynolds (Firefly)*
Loot it by wearing: Khakis, button-down or flannel shirt, black boots, brown trench coat, suspenders

Keep the space-Western flavor of Mal's look with casual, flattering clothes that stick to an earth-shades palette. The suspenders are optional, so rock 'em only if you think you can pull it off (and remember not to wear a belt). For a truly Whedonesque ensemble, you can't beat a brown coat. See my notes about properly fitting trousers (page 108) so you don't get pegged as Captain Tightpants.

The Look: *James T. Kirk (Star Trek)*
Loot it by wearing: Crewneck sweater, dark pants, black shoes

One reason Captain Kirk was such a hit with intergalactic babes: dude knew how to dress. Okay, yes, *technically* he wore a uniform, and you don't want to go walking around with a Starfleet insignia on your chest. But that doesn't mean you can't take some notes from the captain. Choose a solid-colored sweater that's the right size (it should fit across your shoulders without straining or sagging).

The Look: *Tony Stark (Iron Man)*
Loot it by wearing: Well-tailored suits and shirts, classy leather shoes, a devilish grin, perfectly trimmed facial hair

This look is a confident and fun style for the geek with money to spend. Obviously, this is a look more suited to a more formal date setting—unless, like Tony Stark, you don't give a damn what people think of you.

Geek vs. Zits: It's Clobberin' Time!

I'm not playing to stereotypes here, Player One. According to the American Academy of Dermatology, the number of acne sufferers in their twenties, thirties, forties, and beyond—geeks and non-geeks alike—is on the uptick. So, if your skin is more The Thing than Ben Grimm, you're not alone. Nor, I might add, are you without hope.

Washing your face is obviously key to healthy skin: twice a day (no more) and after sweating. Resist the urge to scrub hard—it'll only aggravate your skin. Apply a gentle, non-abrasive cleanser with your fingertips (not a washcloth). Avoid products that contain alcohol, and stay away from toners, astringents, and abrasives. Rinse when you're done, and once you're clean, keep your hands off—you don't want to transfer oil from your fingers to your pores. And don't squeeze or pop blemishes; you're liable to make things worse.

If your skin doesn't improve after a few weeks of a consistent skincare regimen, then it's time to bring in science. A dermatologist can prescribe stronger products, or even medication, to get your skin as eerily smooth as the Silver Surfer's.

GROOMING: A WALKTHROUGH

When you're on that first date, your Player Two is going to spend a lot of time looking at your face. In fact, if you heed our advice on how to dress, you've set your face in a rather charming, well-decked-out frame. So here's how to get your mug looking as hand-some as possible.

Handle the hair ahead of time. If you want to get your hair looking neat and tidy for your date, get it trimmed at least a week in advance. A day-of haircut can be a disaster if the stylist decides to go Edward Scissorhands on you, chopping off way too much and leaving you with a new look that you can't restyle. Get your hair cut on a regular schedule (every six weeks is a good one). If you're look-ing shaggier than Scott Pilgrim and absolutely must get a haircut at the last minute, explain to the stylist that you want it trimmed just enough to look like you didn't go out of your way to get it cut.

 The night of the date is not the time to be popping pimples and picking at your face, either. You do not want gross, oozy, red sores on your face by any means. Pick up some cleanser from the local pharmacy a few days in advance that'll help clear them up, and see "Geeks vs. Zits," opposite, for more skin care tips.

Mind your majestic mane: One more note about your 'do: Weird hair is a huge turnoff for women, and for good reason. You don't want to look like Doc Brown on the outside if you're Marty McFly on the inside. Brush and comb it into place; if you're not sure how best to handle it, get advice from whoever trims it. A little bit of a styling product in your hair can control flyaways and help you get that "bed head" look. Avoid *too much* product (a pea-sized blob is probably enough); you can always add more, but once you've used too much, you're pretty much stuck with it.

Clean up. A shower is always the first step, but don't forget the details. Unless you're Lady Deathstrike in X2, there is no reason for your fingernails to be excessively long. Trim them and keep them clean—because you aren't Dig Dug and you don't spend all day digging through the earth. Dirty nails are a no-go.

Fix your facial hair. If you're the clean-shaven type, shave after a shower since the hot water will soften your skin. Alternately, hold a warm, wet washcloth to your face for thirty seconds before shaving. When you're done shaving, rinse with cold water and use a styptic pencil to close up any nicks. If you wear a beard, don't think that gets you out of daily facial hair maintenance: Use a clipper to tame wild mustache and beard hairs, and use a razor regularly to avoid the dreaded neckbeard. As a rule of thumb, the longer your face, the shorter you should trim your beard. As epic as Alan Moore's beard might be, it's more Rasputin than romantic.

The sweet smell of success: When it comes to cologne, always try before you buy. Pick a scent that reacts well with your body chemistry, and then apply where your body produces heat. Wrists, neck, and chest are each good choices, but apply only at one spot. Women tend to have a more sensitive sense of smell than men, and too much cologne is waaaaay worse than not enough. Ideally, it shouldn't be strong enough for her to notice unless she's close to you (which is the whole point, really).

 Studies have shown that women are particularly attracted to musk and black-licorice smells.

Contrary to what the commercials might tell you, drugstore "body sprays" will not make you a magnet for scantily clad babes—opt for the classy stuff from a department store where a clerk can advise you. Or go without.

Final check: I hate to sound like your mom, but *stand up straight*, Player One—one study showed that how you stand (or slouch) counts for more 80 percent of your date's first impression. So keep your shoulders back and head high, give yourself one last once-over in the mirror, and then give yourself a thumbs-up. You look good.

The Kobayashi Maru: Social Preparation

Starfleet may think it's okay to screw with their cadets by putting them in unwinnable situations. But I wouldn't Kobayashi Maru you like that, Player One. In my version, we're going to review a scenario that *seemed* hopeless, and see what we can learn from it. We'll have to leave Federation Space to do it, though.

In *The 13th Warrior*, the film adaptation of Michael Crichton's *Eaters of the Dead*, an Arab poet named Ahmed ibn Fadlan is exiled to the far north and forced to live with the barbarians known as Norsemen.

Despite the film's shortcomings, *The 13th Warrior* is one of our favorite action-packed popcorn movies. Because of the Vikings. Also, the *Beowulf* references. And, most relevant to our purposes, the material on which it is based (*Beowulf* and the notes from the *real* Ahmed ibn Fadlan) can teach you a lot about developing social skills.

Think about it: a man is thrown into a place where he knows no one, doesn't speak the language, and has to fend for himself. It's very much like going on a first date: you don't really know the person you're with, and while you probably do speak her language, you don't know a whole lot about what she's into and what she wants to talk about. And, for the most part, you're on your own.

As you prepare for an exciting excursion into the unknown, let's absorb these lessons, and prime your social skills in one seriously bad-ass way. The *13th Warrior* way.

Listen Up

Poor Ahmed. He initially has a hard time interacting with the Vikings. But then comes an important moment: One of the Vikings, having insulted the poet's mother, is shocked when the poet returns the insult with an equally brutal quip. Ahmed then explains that he mastered the Viking's entire language—one drastically different from his own—simply by listening to it being spoken. Which would take an amazing, and perhaps implausible, ability to focus and pay attention. Remember to marshal your own listening skills and pay attention to what your Player Two has to say. Nobody doesn't like a good listener.

Don't Be Shy

Throughout his journey, Ahmed is quiet. Closed off. But eventually, he breaks his silence, quits his shyness, and jumps into a conversation when he has something worthwhile to say. This is a valuable lesson, Player One. It's natural to be nervous when conversing with someone new. But you have to push yourself through it. Be prepared to start by asking simple questions, which will show you're engaged in the conversation while still inviting her to do most of the talking.

Make Eye Contact

In *The 13th Warrior*, Ahmed tends to look the wild Norsemen right in the eye when he speaks—particularly at that intense moment when he reveals he can understand them. Making eye contact shows someone that you're interested in what they are saying and that you're a part of the conversation. Don't stare your date down, but do be sure you can make eye contact in a natural, comfortable way.

Be Prepared to Try New Things
One of the biggest issues Ahmed faces in the film is the challenge of embracing a culture that isn't his own.

When the Norsemen's oracle deems that Ahmed needs to accompany the Vikings on their journey, the poet has serious doubts. But they do in fact depend on him, and he becomes a critical part of their team. When he's wounded in the first big battle, a woman tends to his wounds using a treatment he deems filthy. She scoffs and tells him he'll be ill if he doesn't use it. Sure enough, it works.

The point?

It's important to be ready to experience something new when meeting a new person. As Ahmed was quick to learn, the world is a big place, and people are different everywhere you go. If he had judged harshly and left, as was his preference, he would have missed out on a journey that, as he admits ultimately, enriches his life. So approach your date with an open mind, Player One. You may not learn to how to communicate with Vikings, but you'll undoubtedly learn something new about her.

Primp My Ride: How to Get Your Car Date-Ready

The journey may be as important as the destination, Player One, but if the geek canon has taught us anything, it's that awesome transportation goes a long way—and not just literally. But you don't need to be as rich as Bruce Wayne to deck out your own personal Batmobile with all the essential features. Think about Han Solo and the *Millenium Falcon*: "She may not look like much, but she's got it where it counts." Here's a couple tips for keeping your car as cool as KITT (but without that annoying voice).

Toss the trash. Your date shouldn't have to compete for seat space with the detritus of drive-thrus past. Keep a plastic bag on hand for flotsam and jetsam when you're cruising around, and toss it before opening the hatch for a co-pilot.

Kill the crumbs. Even if you're the most fastidious of on-the-go snackers, crumbs, dust, and other sundry gross 'n' crusties have a Tribble-like tendency to be fruitful and multiply in seat cushions and on floors. Bust out a Dustbuster (or pony up a quarter at a car wash) and suck 'em up.

Wax on, wax off. Whether your getaway car has emerged from a rough winter with an exoskeleton of salt stains or is just a little dusty from trundlin' down country roads, it'll definitely look better with a shiny exterior. Loosen dirt's death grip at home by sprinkling the

area with cream of tartar, followed with a round of soap and water, and keep that coveted shine streak free by buffing it dry with a soft towel. No time? Even a quick blast with the hose and a windshield wipe-down at the gas pump will add points for chivalry.

Get fresh. Car smells worse than a wet Ewok? Put down the cardboard pine tree: covering up a bad smell with another smell is just asking for an asthma attack. Soak up spill-related smells with a sprinkle of baking soda (vacuum it after a few hours). Just a general malodorous miasma? Stick a chunk of charcoal (yes, like you grill with) in the car, let it suck up the smell for a few days, and then toss it.

Tweak the control panel. Obviously, you shouldn't take your date out in a car that's missing something crucial like, say, a steering wheel or second seatbelt, but what about minor issues like a wonky wiper blade or a busted CD player (or, worse, tape deck)? Don't sweat it, especially if you can't muster the cash for a big repair. Unless your radio is stuck playing "500 Miles (I'm Gonna Be)" like Marshall's in *How I Met Your Mother* . . . that, you might want to take care of.

CHAPTER 5

First Contact: The Date!

ongratulations, Player One. You've successfully asked out the girl of your dreams. But that move was only the beginning of the game, and now it's time to level up.

Think of this moment as a loading screen: you're psyched, you're nervous, and you're not quite sure what's going to happen next. What if you say the wrong thing? What if she gets bored? What if, after all this preparation and anticipation, you just mess it all up? Game over?

Those pre-screen jitters are perfectly normal. Whether Player Two is someone you've known for a long time or a brand-new acquaintance, nerves before a first date affect everyone. In fact, you should take time to enjoy those feelings of nervous excitement and anticipation, because they're a key part of the game. It's like the opening to, say, Bioshock: "Son, you were born to do great things . . ." You hear those lines (and survive the crash), and you can't help but be excited about what's to come—and wonder how the hell you're going to pull it off.

By Your Command: The Single Cylon's Guide to Dating

So the first date—a goal you've pursued as doggedly and hopefully as the colonial refugees of *Battlestar Galactica* sought Earth—is imminent. And though you may be tempted to, in the words of Admiral Adama, "roll a hard six" and just go for it, you're actually better off engaging the dating process as if you were a Cylon. That's right—the calculating, humanlike machines that are Adama's sworn enemy make pretty good dating role models.

Why? Because Cylons plan ahead. Cylons don't jump into situations without plotting out every possible outcome. And while you aren't a machine (unless the Cylons have indeed finally taken over, in which case I welcome our new robot overlords), you're still going to want to plan your moves. Simply knowing that you're prepared will give you the cool confidence of a cybernetic life form.

Compile your data.

By the time the Cylons show up on your long-range scanners, they already know exactly what their plan is and how it is going to unfurl. Follow their example, Player One, and work out your itinerary in advance. Know where you're going, and how to get there. Consider all the details: Who's driving? Where will you park? If you're taking public transit, do you know how to get to your date from the station or bus stop? Do you need a reservation for wherever you're going? Although Cylons generally keep their plans to themselves, you should communicate with your date so you're both on the same page. (Nothing kills your game faster than a string of "Where are you?," "Where should I wait?," "No, your *other* left" texts.)

The Cylons are articulate and they plan ahead. Strategize about what you want to chat about. Have a couple of interesting topics at the ready, and try not to waste time regaling your date with stories she already knows or discussions you've already had.

Studies show that remembering and recalling personal information in conversations is one of the most effective ways to create a bond—so focus your conversations on what you know about her.

Plan for contingencies.

What if your date hates the restaurant you picked or isn't into the food she ordered? What if she doesn't want to talk about the topics you prepared? Have some backup plans, and think about how you'll improvise if you have to.

If the butterflies in your stomach feel more like pterodactyls, put a hand on your abdomen and take deep breaths to the count of five—a proven technique to conquer anxiety.

Devise an escape route.

Win or lose, every warrior needs an exit strategy. In *Battlestar Galactica*, the easiest retreat was to fire up the FTL drive and jump to another location. Unfortunately, we don't have the technology to do that IRL just yet. But you should think about the different ways your date might play out. How will you get home? What if (score!) your date wants to come *with* you—or if she wants you to go with her? Consider all the possibilities (even the implausibly great ones and the disastrously unlikely ones) and plan how you will respond in each situation.

Consider previous first dates.

"All of this has happened before, and all of it will happen again."
So says the Cycle of Time scroll. Even though it might open up old
wounds, it's important to think about what you've done on dates in
the past. What worked for you? What went wrong? What could you
do differently? How will this time be different?

Stay in touch with your human side.

As admirable as the Cylon approach to event planning may be,
there is a difference between having a plan and scripting your date.
Go ahead and lay things out and have a specific idea of where to go
and what to talk about, but don't insist that events proceed exactly
according to your calculations. You don't want your date thinking
you're a robot, after all.

Geek Psych-Up Mix Tape

While it might be a little early in *our* relationship to be swapping mix tapes, I feel like . . . like . . . oh, I don't know, like we've known each other forever. You know what I mean?

Okay, but seriously. You're getting ready. You've got an hour or two before it's time to hit the town. While you're busy fussing over yourself in the mirror or picking out your favorite outfit, listen to these songs to pumped yourself up.

1. "The Final Countdown" by Europe: It's almost impossible to hear this song without picturing Will Arnett's character on *Arrested Development* dancing around, waving knives in front of his face, and accidentally shooting out lighter fluid instead of birds. G.O.B. Bluth may be an unbelievably selfish twit, but the man exudes confidence—maybe it'll rub off on you while you rock out.

2. "Bohemian Rhapsody" by Queen: If you don't start head-banging during the bridge, either you're doing it wrong or you've never watched *Wayne's World* . . . which is doing it wrong.

3. "Halo Theme Mjolnir Mix" from the *Halo 2 Original Soundtrack*: The music in Halo is the perfect example of why some game soundtracks sell a ton of copies. While all of the orchestrated music in Halo is epic and sweeping, it's the powerful theme song that works best as a pump-up anthem. And thanks to the incredible guitar licks by Steve Vai, it's not just a great theme song, it's one of the most epic theme songs ever.

4. "Duel of the Fates" from *Star Wars Episode I*: Okay, okay. The Star Wars prequels are, for the most part, pretty damn terrible. But there is no denying that the light saber battle between Qui-Gon Jinn, Obi-Wan Kenobi, and Darth Maul is awesome. And what's even better is the music accompanying it. This is the only classical song to ever have a video debut on MTV's *Total Request Live,* because it is awesome.

5. "Battle without Honor or Humanity" by Tomoyasu Hotei: Don't recognize the name? This is the theme song from *Kill Bill.* Now try not to hear the trumpets: *ba-ba-BA!* You can't do it. But what you can do is own this date like the Bride pwned her many nemeses on her quest for revenge. (No katana on your first date, though, even if it's a Hattori Hanzo sword. Unless that date is with Bill.)

6. "Eye of the Tiger" by Survivor: Because, *Rocky.*

7. "Dragonborn" from Skyrim: The sweet sounds of a 90-man barbarian choir singing in Draconic, the nonexistent runic-alphabet language from the game, get gamers psyched to battle dragons. It'll absolutely get you psyched to walk out the door.

8. "Wake Up" by Rage Against the Machine: You might not recognize it outside the film it shines in, *The Matrix,* but this slightly obscure pick still totally rages.

9. "Glory of Love" covered by New Found Glory: I'm not saying that the original by Peter Cetera isn't good. 'Cause it is. But NFG's cover, with fast-driving power chords and catchy pop-punk-infused harmonies, turns this adult contemporary song from the *Karate Kid, Part II* soundtrack into a fun, energetic track.

10. "The Legend of Zelda Theme" by Koji Kondo: In this young boy's quest to save a girl, there's one stirring, epic song that accompanies all his many adventures. It's impossible to listen to this theme, penned by one of the greatest video game composers of all time, and not picture yourself holding up a tiny, 8-bit orange sword and starting your adventure.

11. "Through the Fire and the Flames" by Dragonforce: Do you know how many bands in history have tunes so epic that they are a boss level in a video game? Just this one. Dragonforce's guitar shredding and impossible solos will absolutely get you psyched. (You may get flashbacks to control-throwing rage with *Guitar Hero II*. Be careful.)

12. "Still Alive" by Jonathan Coulton: While JoCo's song from the original *Portal* is neither an arena-rock anthem nor or an intro to an epic battle scene, it's exactly the kind of song that will help you relax before a date and get you smiling.

13. The entire *Tron: Legacy* soundtrack by Daft Punk: You're welcome.

14. "Sorairo Days" by Shoko Nakagawa: The theme song to the anime series *Gurren Lagann* is a surefire way to get yourself psyched, not so much for the music as for a reminder of what the show is about: giant robots *powered by manliness*. The series starts with mankind trapped underground and ends with robots the size of galaxies throwing nebulas at one another. Figure *that* out.

Choose Your Own Adventure: A First Date Simulation

Three's a crowd, Player One, so I won't be going with you on your big night out. Nevertheless, it is dangerous to go alone. So to get you ready, we're going to utilize the holodeck that is your brain to engage in a bit of a practice run.

You can think of a date as a real-life "Choose Your Own Adventure" book. The right choices will lead you to more dates, and maybe a future, with someone you're into. Choosing the wrong path gets you flattened under a boulder, or catapulted off a cliff, or dropped into a bottomless pit or, even worse, doomed to have no second date. You won't be able to flip back to the beginning of the date when you've realize you made a wrong decision, but you can avoid some common pitfalls by working your way through the simulation below.

You're the star of the story. Let's go!

 Saying your date's name once or twice in the first few minutes is an easy way to boost your connection with her—just don't go overboard.

LEVEL 1

You and your date have met up at last, and you're getting settled into whatever awesome activity you've picked: checking out animatronic dinosaurs, strapping on laser-tag vests, settling in for cocktails before you both experience molecular gastronomy for the first time.

She turns to you expectantly, and you realize it's time to talk. You open your mouth and . . .

1. Start talking about yourself right away.

2. Talk about something easy, like the weather.

3. Ask questions about where she's traveled, what she does with her friends, what she studied in school, or what she does for a living.

Results:

1. She smiles politely while she listens, but her eyes look a little glazed-over. When you finally stop talking, she takes up the conversation after a long pause, like she didn't realize it was even her turn to talk.

Of course you should talk about yourself . . . just not too much. Don't be the kind of tiresome windbag who never lets his date get a word in edgewise.

GAME OVER

2. Your date stares at you for a minute and then mutters something to the effect of "Yeah . . . I guess I like sunshine."

Weather chitchat is where conversation goes to die. Are you in an elevator or something? Don't do small talk. Go big or go home. Which means only talk about meteorology if you're in The Day After Tomorrow*–like conditions.*

GAME OVER

3. She instantly perks up and launches into a hilarious anecdote about getting lost with her friends—in *Japan*. Wait a minute, this girl is *awesome*.

People love to talk about themselves, and most people have great travel tales or stories from their school days. Talk about favorite places, classes, books, hobbies. Women, more than men, form social bonds over similarities, so don't hesitate to point out all the stuff you've got in common with your date.

ADVANCE TO LEVEL 2

LEVEL 2

Now that you've covered some basic ground, it's time to really get to know each other. So when a lull in the conversation hits, you decide to . . .

1. Delve into deeper stuff to prove you're a man of substance: politics, religious beliefs, her parents, her dating history.

2. Start educating her all about your main geek hobby to show that you're passionate about something.

3. Ask a random question: "Wouldn't it be exciting to just . . . give everything up and explore the world in a sailboat?"

Results:

1. Your date looks a little uncomfortable, mentions a few things, and then tries to change the subject.

If this person is the One—and by One I mean soul mate, not some hacker Morpheus is looking for—you'll eventually have to discuss these things at length. But there's no reason to jump into them right away, especially on a first date.

GAME OVER

2. You watch your date's smile dissolve into nothing as you launch into an epic tirade about the sexual politics of Rogue and Gambit.

Unless you met this girl on a panel about comic books or she is wearing an "I Heart Judge Dredd" T-shirt, avoid discussing your primary geek passion to the exclusion of all else. Yes, this is a big part of who you are, but remember, it isn't the sum total of who you are.

GAME OVER

3. Your date laughs, considers the question, and answers truthfully. Soon you're both engaged in an intense debate on the merits of water-based travel. You'd never really thought about it before, but now you're both cracking up.

Contrary to popular belief, a good way to find out your date's beliefs is to ask her questions that have nothing to do with her beliefs at all. If you both have similar answers, it bodes well for long-term compatibility. Some examples to try:

➤ *"Choose one: power of flight or power of invisibility?"*
➤ *"If you needed bail money, who would you call?"*
➤ *"If scientists could pinpoint the exact date of your death, would you want to know it?"*
➤ *"If you could time travel just once, where and when would you visit?"*
➤ *"What's the best meal you've ever had?"*

Fire away, Player One.
ADVANCE TO LEVEL 3

LEVEL 3

You've had a great date—conversation was sparkling, food was great, dinosaurs were Jurass-tastic, and lasers were tagged. And now it's time to pay the bill. Your date offers to split it, so you . . .

1. Insist on paying the whole thing. You're a gentleman, after all—no matter if she wants to go halvsies or not.
2. Say okay, but the next one's on you. Then let her pay half.
3. Say okay, but the next one's on you. Then let her pay. All of it.

Results:
1. Your date feebly tries to cover her half a few more times, and you wave her off. Chivalry isn't dying on your watch! Besides, who wouldn't like having a free dinner? She's got to be grateful, right?

When in doubt, pay. But be careful, Player One: though you should absolutely be prepared to cover the full cost of your first date, everyone reacts differently to this convention. Some girls will find it sweet and considerate, while others might worry that you're expecting something (as in, somethin' something) in return. Be attentive and respect your date's feelings above all else.

ADVANCE TO LEVEL 4

2. Both of you toss in enough cash to cover the cost. You gallantly offer to foot the tip and tax, and your date agrees without complaint.

It's the New Millenium, Player One. The Internet is lightning fast, the Higgs Boson is within our grasp, and women are outearning men. That is to say, if your date suggests it, there's nothing wrong with splitting a check. A little chivalry doesn't hurt, though, and the gesture of covering the last little bit will mean a lot.

ADVANCE TO LEVEL 4

3. Your date pauses, frowns, and asks if you're joking. You're not. You mumble an answer, but she's too pissed off to hear. She plunks down a couple twenties and storms off faster than you can say "let's do this again sometime!"

Seriously, dude, don't give a girl the impression that she's nothing more than a meal ticket. Pony up at least your fair share, if not the whole bill.

GAME OVER

LEVEL 4

You and your date have paused on the sidewalk after the main event, the conversation's winding down, and now the moment is here. You want to give the evening an ending that's as memorable as the end of *The Usual Suspects* or *Fight Club* (though without explosions or the revelation that you're a sociopathic criminal mastermind), so naturally you . . .

1. Make a fast physical move, like grabbing her hand or leaning in towards her with a gleam in your eye. After that, instinct will take over.

2. Realize that, *whoa*, you've had a few Pan-Galactic Gargle-Blasters too many. You try to focus, but things are a bit . . . off-kilter. Since when does your date have two blurry heads?

3. Keep the action at a Clark Kent level. Casually ask about her future plans, the movie or museum she talked about, or that new boutique or neighborhood she wanted to explore.

Results:

1. Your date looks startled and pulls away. She says she'll call you, and then heads off in the opposite direction, and you're left wondering if she really meant it or if this is the first *and* last contact you'll have with her.

Unless your date was going spectacularly well earlier on, you really shouldn't rush into physical contact, like hand-holding or a first kiss. Nothing is worse than forcing First Contact (unless we're talking about Star Trek: First Contact—*if she doesn't want to watch that, it's her loss, because that movie is awesome). Point being: don't force it.*

GAME OVER

2. You can't seem to figure out how to get home, much less what to do with your date. Though she doesn't seem thrilled about it, she offers you a ride, drops you off . . . and drives away without a second glance.

If you drink too much on your first date, not only will you give a horrible first impression, you also won't be able to drive home. This doesn't just apply to alcohol, either; also know how much sugar and caffeine you can tolerate.

GAME OVER

3. Your date is thrilled that you remembered the things she had brought up, and suddenly you've got the perfect in. You ask her to hang out next weekend, and she agrees. Date Number Two is a go.

When the date goes well, don't be afraid to suggest going out again. If the body language was right and the signals were all there, go for it. Be specific, be direct, and if you say you're going to "call her later," then actually call her later. After that, if things are still looking good, and your date is still looking good, maybe it's time for the first kiss.

CONGRATULATIONS! A WINNER IS YOU!
TO BE CONTINUED . . .

Extra Credits: Post-Date Easter Eggs

Needless to say, Player One, sometimes the date doesn't end when the check is paid. Sometimes things keep getting better—or worse. Here are some tips for handling the bonus materials (score!) or negotiating the wreckage (better luck next time).

KISSING 101

I'm hesitant to even tell you these things, Player One, because nothing will wreck a kiss faster than trying to remember some predetermined sequence of steps while you're in the middle of a liplock. This isn't the Konami code here, and trying to make out according to those directions (Up Up Down Down Left Right Left Right) would only make things weird. And anyway, the first kiss is more about the promise of things to come than about perfect technique. So all you have to do is avoid a critical failure, and these simple tactics will prevent that every time.

1. Look into her eyes. (You'll reflexively close your eyes during the actual kiss, which is fine.) Depending on the situation, you might place a hand gently on her cheek, or pull her close to you in an embrace.

2. Tilt your head to the side.

3. Move closer, slowly but decisively. Hesitation may cause you to lose the moment. If she's not up for it, she'll let you know.

4. Purse your lips and gently touch them to hers. Kiss softly at first, opening your lips wider if she responds in kind. Let your tongue dart out to touch her lips. If she kisses back harder, ramp up the passion. If she pulls away, hit pause and let her make the next move.

The League of Extraordinary Gentlemen

Knights, quests, and jousts may be relegated to fantasy realms these days, but that doesn't mean chivalry is dead. It's still important to be a gentleman, Player One (and if you can be an extraordinary one, so much the better). And no, Jackie Treehorn, that doesn't mean treating women as if they're fragile objects that need to be shielded from harm. Rather, it means setting yourself apart from the creeps, Neanderthals, and morlocks who populate her world when she's not with you. You're a geek, Player One, and that means you need to be a more evolved specimen of man. Here's how.

Be on time. Think about all the disasters in the geek canon that could have been averted if only the protagonist had been on time. If Peter Parker was able to manage his time in *Spider-Man 2*, maybe things wouldn't have gone so poorly with him at school, at work, and with Mary Jane. If Luke hadn't taken so long getting back from Ben Kenobi's, maybe his aunt and uncle wouldn't have become barbecue. And what if Spock hadn't missed his window of time to save the Romulan homeworld? Sure, the plot twists lead to adventure and exciting times for the audience, but being late leaves the hero emotionally and physically stressed. Take a tip: Be punctual. Better yet, show up a little early.

Mind the little things. The most romantic scene in Cameron Crowe's *Say Anything*? Forget the iconic tableau in which Lloyd Dobler holds up a boombox outside Diane Court's house and blasts Peter Gabriel's "In Your Eyes." Scratch the whole "I gave her my heart, she gave me a pen" bit. No, shy Lloyd captures beautiful Diane's heart with a small gesture: he helps her step over a pile of broken glass in the street. It's something small, sure, but she remembers it, swooning over the moment while telling her father about Lloyd. Broken glass or no, you can be similarly chivalrous by opening doors, pulling out chairs, and walking on the street side of the sidewalk. Trust me, she'll notice.

Be respectful. *Con Air*, while not exactly an Oscar-worthy piece of cinema, is one hell of a fun, action-packed, and often unintentionally hilarious movie. Nicolas Cage's character, convict Cameron Poe, is actually an old-fashioned gentleman who was jailed for defending his woman's honor. When the convicts hijack a plane, Poe takes great care to protect Sally, a guard who is harassed by a very filthy inmate. By great care, I mean he pummels the dirtbag again and again while saying "YOU. DON'T. TREAT. WOMEN. LIKE. THAT." Here's hoping you don't have to pound anybody to a pulp to make your point. But do check in with your inner Nicolas Cage from time to time, to make sure he approves of how you act towards the woman you're with.

TEASER TRAILER: A BRIEF GUIDE TO A STICKY SUBJECT

Sex isn't likely to be a factor on the first date—and in most cases, it probably shouldn't be (more about that in a moment). Nevertheless, we both know it's on your mind, so it's not too soon to start thinking about it (I don't mean fantasizing, I'm sure you've been doing lots of that already). Once the relationship gets serious (see chapters 6 and 7), sex—and related topics, like staying over—becomes an even bigger deal, so you need to be ready. Nothing personal, but I don't really want to be in the bedroom with the two of you, Player One. So here are some guidelines you should acquaint, or reacquaint, yourself with. Close the door and I'll just show myself out.

1. **Forget about first-date sex.** Yeah, it happens on TV all the time, but those sitcoms only have 22 minutes to tell a story. Just because your date's going well doesn't mean you should expect to end up under the sheets by midnight. You don't know each other well enough to be swapping DNA. (If this is someone you already know, and you have a shared history of mutual trust, *maybe* it's an option. But reframing your friendship towards romance is tricky enough without jumping right into the sack.)

2. **If she's not ready, honor that.** And if you're not ready, say so. Just because you're a dude doesn't mean you have to be the one who's overeager.

3. **Have the talk.** Sorry, but this is life in the twenty-first century: You need to be frank with each other about any past or present STDs and your HIV status. If you think this is an awkward conversation to have on a first date, you're right. Which is one more reason to wait till you're more comfortable with each other before doing the deed. Also be clear about protection in advance of things heating up; once the clothes start coming off, it's not easy to make smart decisions about contraception.

4. Be her guest. Staying the night isn't just a matter of convenience; it strengthens your connection and brings you together emotionally. If you're at her place, respect the house rules, and *no snooping*. If she's staying at yours, make her feel welcome and comfortable.

FINAL TROUBLESHOOTING: HOW TO FIX OR PREVENT 12 SIGNIFICANT DATING MALFUNCTIONS

Maybe—hopefully—you'll never encounter this dirty dozen of dating dilemma. But even so, knowing the solutions will boost your confidence.

I suspect my date may be a man (and I'm not cool with that).
Signs of masked masculinity include hair on your date's knuckles, hands, and forearms. Check for a prominent Adam's apple (perhaps covered by a scarf or turtleneck). Check to see if your date's shoulders are broader than her hips.

My date may be a con artist.
Be wary if your date asks for a short-term loan or investment money, won't tell you her last name, or often changes her stories and claims.

I'm dating someone I work with.
Find out the company policy about dating coworkers. Avoid telling colleagues and avoid all physical contact in the workplace. Don't use workplace e-mails for nonbusiness communications. Never arrive or depart together.

I'm dating a vampire.
Insist on separate sleeping arrangements. Spend time together during dawn and dusk. Skip the garlic knots.

My zipper's stuck.
Pull the stuck fabric taut, holding it so the zipper is away from your body. Guide the zipper down with your free hand, using steady force. Pull—but don't yank—to avoid a *There's Something about Mary* frank-and-beans situation.

My B.O. is off the charts.
If you can't excuse yourself to duck into a pharmacy and buy deodorant, go into a restroom and wash under your arms with paper towels, hot water, and a bit of soap. Dry thoroughly before re-dressing. If excessive sweating is an ongoing problem, consider keeping extra shirts handy for now and seeing your doctor later—he or she can prescribe you stronger stuff than drugstore products.

I have skunkbreath.
Chew some gum or mints that you wisely brought with you on the date. (Two minutes of gum chewing is enough.) Or ask a waiter or bartender for a piece of gum, some parsley, or a cinnamon stick to chew. Failing that, rinse your mouth with water several times, rinsing-and-spitting as if you were at the dentist's.

I spilled wine or food on her.
Do not attempt to wipe up the stain; supply her with a damp napkin that she can use to blot it up. Apologize and offer to pay the dry cleaning bill. Order another glass of wine—for her.

She owns a maniac dog.
Meet the dog on neutral ground first, like a nearby park. Approach the animal in a low-key manner, avoiding eye contact, and don't pet the animal until it's relaxed and friendly. Feed the dog some treats. If you plan on frequent visits, lend your lady a hat or shirt to take home so the dog can get used to your scent.

My credit card was declined.
Excuse yourself from the table and ask to see the manager. Explain that you're on a date and that you'd like to handle the situation quietly. Ask if you can leave your driver's license or other collateral and return with the payment later. Call your credit card company and ask for a temporary credit extension, just enough to cover the cost of the meal. Or call a friend or family member who might bring you some funds.

I can't remove her bra.
Most bras have a hook-and-eye clasp in the back; the hooks will be on her right. Reach behind her with your right hand and bend your index finger over the clasp, slipping your finger between the fabric and her skin. Hold your thumb against the eye side of the clasp and push the hook side towards your thumb with your index or middle finger. Alternately, squeeze thumb and fingers, bringing the eyes and hooks towards each other. The clasp may pop open at that point, or you may have to guide the hooks out of place with a finger. When it's done, slide the bra off her arms. Note: This is much easier, if not as suave, if you use two hands; stand in front of her, reach back and grasp one side of the clasp with each hand; pull hook and eyes towards each other and then unhook.

I get the feeling that I'm boring the crap out of her.
Signs that she's interested in what you're saying include sustained eye contact, smiling, and mirroring some of your own gestures and posture. If she leans towards you, touches her hair, licks her lips, or briefly touches or pats you as you talk, those are very good signs. Remember that if you don't know each other very well, she (and you) may start off with more standoffish body language. That's normal. What you want to see is a shift towards more animated, energetic, and relaxed behavior. If the signs don't seem to

be in your favor, try talking about similarities the two of you have. Reference anything that she's told you about herself, which shows you've been paying attention. Be sure to use her name in the conversation, which fosters connection. If nothing's working, ask some questions so she can talk for a while.

CHAPTER 6

Beyond Thunderdome: The Day After, and Beyond

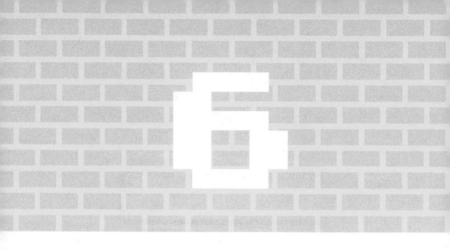

 our alarm goes off. Little bits of sunshine stream in through your bedroom window, glimmering like rays off the Triforce. You sleepily reach for your phone before anything else, as is traditional for all respectable geeks. You turn it on, and your day officially begins.

Player One, welcome to the morning after a first date.

What happens next depends on how thing went previous night went. Don't panic—or, okay, maybe panic a little. Just keep it proportional. Here are some possible scenarios, from "Impressive . . . most impressive" to "I find your lack of faith . . . disturbing."

Code Green: There are a bunch of texts waiting for you from your date, all about how much fun she had and how she can't wait to see you again.

Response: Smile, wipe the sleep from your eyes, and craft a charming, witty response saying something similar. Possibly with some emoticons. Check your totem to make sure you're not in an *Inception*-type dream world.

Code Blue: You open up Facebook and Twitter and see that she's posted something vague, but still positive: happy song lyrics, a cute LOLcat, a little ASCII heart.

Response: Get on with your day, whistling a happy tune and keeping an eye on your inbox. Give her a call or send a message in a few hours if you haven't heard from her first.

Code Yellow: The date went fine, but in the morning, there's nothing. No text, no message on Facebook, no tweets.

Response: Okay, maybe you misread the situation. Or maybe she's wondering why *you* haven't sent any signals yet. No need to stay cloaked, Player One. Go ahead and send a short and sweet hello—nothing too whiny—just to let her know what a great time you had. Then find stuff to keep yourself busy so you won't spend the next eight hours watching for a response. (This might be a good day to alphabetize that three-month stack of comics and get them in longboxes.)

Code Orange: There are zero texts. Her Facebook status is something depressing, like a frowny emoticon or the lyrics to a Dashboard Confessional song.

Response: You remember some details from the night before: you were 47 minutes late, she kept calling you Steve even though your name is Thundarr . . . Okay, go ahead, put your phone down, bury your head in your pillow. Then cook yourself some eggs for breakfast and head to a buddy's house for some soul-cleansing Xbox action.

Code Red: There's a text and . . . it ain't a happy one. She totally slams you, saying she had the worst date in the history of dating. On Facebook, Twitter, Foursquare, even MySpace (thorough!), she's ranting about how creepy you are.

Response: You could attack back, causing a social media disaster and perhaps exploding the entire Internet. But take the high road,

Player One. Thank her for her time and break off all communication, and then get some supportive friends together for a Blu-ray movie marathon. (And if her social media sniping doesn't flare down, complain to the authorities that she's violating her TOS agreement.)

What happens next? Fear not, Player One. There are proper ways to navigate every single one of these situations. And much like multiple dimensions in comic books, there are endless possibilities for how things may turn out. So get ready. Even if you didn't find the Ark of the Covenant right away, there are plenty of other crates in the warehouse. Your days of playing a solo campaign are coming to an end.

Game Over? How to Respawn After You're Fragged

So you took a chance, asked her out, gave it your all, put your best foot forward . . . and now you feel like you barely escaped a Reaver attack. Maybe it's better to stick to the core planets and leave the frontiers of dating to the browncoats, independents, and other hardier stock?

I can understand why a bad date might disrupt your serenity, Player One (ouch, that was bad). Let's abandon the *Firefly* references in favor of a different space saga. In the 1999 film *Galaxy Quest*, Commander Peter Quincy Taggart, played by actor Jason Nesmith, who in turn is played by real-life actor Tim Allen (get all that?), has an awesome, omnipresent catchphrase: "Never give up. Never surrender."

Inspiring, right? Well, sort of. In *Galaxy Quest*, Nesmith becomes famous for his portrayal of Taggart. Unfortunately, after the cult TV series ends, he has a hard time finding new roles. He relies on conventions and other public appearances to generate income; the rest of his "crew" resents the attention he gets and how much he seems to enjoy it. In other words, they're tired of hearing him shout that catchphrase—to them, it's anything but inspiring. You may feel the same way when friends or family try to encourage you after a dating disaster by employing one of these clichés:

> ➤ "There are plenty of fish in the sea."
> ➤ "Your time will come."
> ➤ "Time heals all wounds."
> ➤ "If it's meant to be, it's meant to be."
> ➤ "She doesn't deserve you."

While lines like this are meant to be comforting, they can do more harm than good . . . or just raise more questions and doubt. When *is* my time? How long *will* it take until I get over it? Who *does* that person deserve, if not me? And why are you comparing me to a fish, anyway?

So politely thank whoever is handing you those lines (they really are trying to make you feel better, after all), and keep in mind the number one rule for dealing with post-date depression syndrome: *Keep yourself in play.*

Consider the example of Jeffrey Dexter Boomhauer III, aka Boomhauer, from *King of the Hill*. It's not until the sixth season that we're finally privy to the secret of the character's epic string of successes with women: he never stops trying. Before the puzzled and slightly horrified eyes of young Bobby Hill, Boomhauer attempts to pick up about a dozen women in the span of a minute, barely blinking as he's shot down again and again. You, Player One, are not nearly so obnoxious and shallow, but it's true that success often requires repeated failed attempts. Thomas Edison put it this way: "Many of life's failures are people who did not realize how close they were to success when they gave up."

Luckily, in life as in RPGs, you'll always resurrect after a bad dating encounter. The respawn time will vary, but the important thing is to be mature about the whole thing, avoid any unnecessary nerd raging, and (of course) refer to the previous chapters of this book to get you started with someone new. Here's a guide to how long it may take to bind your wounds and get back on the warhorse.

SHE WAS A STRANGER

Respawn time: 1–2 days

So she doesn't want to see you again romantically? No big deal. This person wasn't really connected to you anyway. If she wants to be friends, great. Go for friendship, if you think you want and will be able to handle that. Plenty of people meet on dating websites like OkCupid only to come to the mutual realization that they make better friends than romantic partners.

SHE WAS AN ACQUAINTANCE

Respawn time: 4–10 days

Here's where things get a little trickier. In the event your date is someone in your circle of friends, a person you see from time to time, it's important to be cool even if the date was a living hell. After all, you might see her again, and she might even end up dating someone you know. Be mature. Don't delete her from Facebook, unfollow her on Twitter, or bash her to your friends. All that reflects poorly on you, and it's negative publicity that might influence other women you'd like to date.

SHE WAS A FRIEND

Respawn time: 1 week to . . . a long time

Ah, the most challenging of the failed dates: the friend. She was someone you've been close to for a while, and the two of you finally decided *hey, let's do this*. If a second date is off the table, try to react the same way you would with an acquaintance. Your lag time before respawn will be a little longer in this case, but you can help speed it along with some concrete closure. You're friends with her and you see her often, so open a channel of communication to find out why it didn't work. Get a reason, accept it, and move on. If things are weird, that's normal. Understand that space might be needed, and if it's you who needs the space, make that clear as well. Saving the friendship is important.

00154 THE GEEK'S GUIDE TO DATING CH 06

Game On! First Moves after a Good (or Great) Date

A round of Capture the Flag in *Halo*, or rolling dice for some tabletop D&D action—those are good games, Player One, and we're all for them (big surprise, right?). But emotional games, head games . . . those games aren't fun at all. So disabuse yourself of the notion that you're in some kind of mental chess match with your Player Two, trying to guess her gambit while keeping your own strategies hidden. You should be in co-op mode, not PvP. Here's how to keep the game going:

PRESS CONTINUE

Don't stand there watching the screen count down (*Continue?* 5 . . . 4 . . . 3 . . . 2 . . .). Go ahead and plunk in the next quarter. Forget all the rules you think you know: call three days after the day, text five days after the date, wait until the sun is eclipsed before leaving a message on Facebook, summon Cthulhu during the harvest moon and dial her number from a pay phone, etc. All of this is nonsense. If you like someone, you go for it. End of story. Give your date a call the next day (or if things went really well, be bold and drop her a text that same night to say so), and suggest going out again. Let her know you had a great time and you're interested in seeing her again. By the way, you don't need to have the next rendezvous planned out before calling her—you can work that out later (which gives you another excuse to call her). I'll have some next-date suggestions for you later in this chapter.

WATCH THE CUTSCENES

If the two of you are already connected through social networks, there's nothing wrong checking to see if she's mentioned you on one of her profiles. But just as you can't interact with NPCs during a video game's cutscene, you should resist the urge to join in on any of those conversations. Don't message her on Twitter about your date or leave comments on her Facebook wall. For all you know, she may have forgotten that you can see her posts. You'll run the risk of putting her on the spot in front of all her friends and followers, some of whom may also be colleagues and networking acquaintances. Even worse, it'll paint you as pushy and invasive. Communicate with her directly, and save the social media crosstalk until you know each other better.

REMEMBER TO RE-RENDER

Just like loading screens give a game time to load the next stage's assets from the disc into the system memory, the time between dates is your chance to make sure you're ready to move forward. Don't just rehash (or obsess over) what was good and bad on your date— take some time to clean up that stream of photos of you and your ex-girlfriend on Facebook, take your good armor to the dry cleaner, and revaluate what *you* want. Revisiting some of this book's earlier chapters may help. Now that you know her better, does Level 2 Dating seem more like a possibility? Is she a Medic, or more like a Rogue? Is she a bigger geek than you thought, or should you save the trip to Kolossal Komix for the third date? And speaking of the next date . . .

Avoiding the Sequel Slump: Making Your Second Date Awesomer

So you've secured the rights to the next date—which I suggest entitling something awesome like *First Date II: Date Harder*. This follow-up to the original will set the stage for whether or not all this dating will turn into a profitable franchise for all involved parties, and hopefully it will be well received by the critics (or at least the only critic that matters, i.e., her).

Unfortunately, in dating as in movies, there's always the risk of the dreaded sophomore slump. Hype builds, fans get super excited, people show up to the premiere wearing kick-ass homemade costumes…and the thing totally flops.

Nobody wants to experience the *Matrix Reloaded* of dating.

Planning that second date has everything to do with how the first date went. If it went well, and you've been talking or texting fairly regularly since, chances are a superior second date is in the cards. Maybe you even suggested it at the end of the first date. But let's not take anything for granted. Here's what you need to do make sure your sequel blows the original out of the water.

USE LESS TECHNOLOGY

Did you meet online? Through a dating website or via social networks? Great, you're a modern dater. But as you may recall from *every sequel released since Facebook was invented*, nothing's more exhausting than an aggressive online campaign trying to build hype around a burgeoning franchise.

Before you cry "But it's called *social* media!," think of it this way: how many times have you found your desire to see a new movie peter out after enduring weeks and weeks of incessant Internet hinting on Facebook, Twitter, or Reddit? In the run-up to your second date, a little mystery goes a long way. Step back from the texting, the frequent likes, and the "flirty" retweets, and save your stories for meatspace. Instead, allow the anticipation—both hers and yours— to build like a carefully orchestrated guerilla marketing campaign.

MAINTAIN INTEREST

It doesn't matter how good the sequel is: the longer it lags behind the original, the less interest there will be (and the fewer butts end up in theater seats on opening weekend). Similarly, while you want to avoid communicating too much, it is important to maintain a connection. You don't want her to think you've forgotten about her. Try doing something absolutely crazy . . . like using your phone *as a phone*. Call her to set up the date and work out arrangements. Chat briefly to keep in touch between dates. But save the long, engaging conversations for your next face-to-face. Texts now and again are fine, but as mentioned above, don't go overboard.

PLAN SOMETHING UNCONVENTIONAL

Nothing makes a franchise feel stale faster than a sequel that isn't really a sequel (three *Hobbit* movies? We're looking at you, Peter Jackson.). You don't need to go to outrageous lengths to impress your date on the second outing, but you shouldn't devolve into just making garlic bread either, Scott Pilgrim. Find a nice in-between, balancing the overly romantic with the utterly simple. Need some second date suggestions? Read on.

Zen and the Art of Second Date-enance

Let's consider the Materia system in *Final Fantasy VII*.

In this classic RPG, Materia is a form of Lifestream, which is the spiritual energy of the world and which powers just about everything. Using Materia, characters can do a number of things. They can enhance their own abilities, adding additional strength or magic, or enhance their weaponry, gaining all sorts of magical capabilities (summoning creatures into battle, casting spells, you name it). The point is, combining different crystals with your weapons and armor enables you to create something better than the original item. The same thing applies when you're working on that second date. Take something basic (Simple Materia), combine it with something a little more romantic (Romantic Materia), to create that perfect second date. **Note:** To my knowledge there is no "Romantic Materia" in *Final Fantasy VII*, or any subsequent games. If there were, it might have made those long love stories a little easier to navigate!

THE GAMING PICNIC

Romantic Materia: picnic, long talks
Simple Materia: games, comic books

While the idea of a picnic date immediately brings to mind checkered white-and-red blankets and wicker baskets, it doesn't have to be that traditional. After all, you're a geek. Bring a deck of playing cards—hell, a deck of *Magic: the Gathering* cards. Bring a pair of PS Vitas. Hit up your favorite comic book shop beforehand on New Book Day, and gather some favorite issues. Invite your geek gal to bring hers as well. Read, talk, game, snack . . . you'll have plenty to do while getting to know one another.

THE AT-HOME MINI FILM FESTIVAL

Romantic Materia: home-cooked meal, long talks, possible cuddling

Simple Materia: DVDs, Blu-rays, streaming channels, popcorn

Chances are, during your first date, you talked about movies, television, and other bits of pop culture. Why not queue up a bunch of those flicks you discussed, maybe introduce your date to films she hasn't seen, and enjoy a little movie marathon? If you've got a good handle on her tastes, you can try surprising her with selections you think she'll like. Or ask for her input and co-curate the perfect quadruple feature. If you include some favorites you have both already seen, you'll be able to talk and continue to get to know one another while watching.

THE BARCADE HANGOUT

Romantic Materia: cocktails, long talks

Simple Materia: arcade games

Those magical bars that also happen to have arcade machines inside make for an excellent first, second, or three-hundredth date. Not only do you have the option to pick up fancy drinks and chat at the bar, there are arcade games for the two of you to conquer together. Bring a roll of quarters and prepare to lock and load for some *Time Crisis III* action.

The Brave and the Bold: Casual Dating

Remember when, in Chapter 1, we discussed knowing what's important to you in a relationship? This is when all of that is going to start to have real meaning, Player One. Because now, you're in a position to start defining things and figuring out just what this new relationship you're building is and where you want it to go.

The term "casual dating" often gets a bad rep, especially due to dating websites with names like OnlineBootyCall.com. Let's be clear right now: casual dating is nothing like "casual encounters," at least by our definition. It doesn't involve impersonal hook-ups, clandestine meetings in bus-station restrooms, grainy cam-to-cam conversations, or phony "business trips" to Houston. It's more about spending time with another person without any commitments or guarantees of a long-term relationship. To use a terrible dating cliché, you're playing the field and figuring out what sort of person you fit with best.

Which is not to say that casual dating rules out something more serious. Often it's a natural step in an evolving relationship, a period of time when the two of you try to determine whether something more than casual is on the horizon. It's a lot like role-playing in an online forum—you can experiment with different parts of your character and see what fits with other people without worry about sustaining something for a long time.

 Casual doesn't mean shallow. Studies have shown that even in casual dating, internal qualities like personality and intelligence are still more important for compatibility than external ones like physical appearance or social status.

There are a number of valid reasons why casual dating might the right fit for you:

You're Not Quite Ready Yet
Lots of geeks use role-playing forums to practice their writing and

hone their characterization skills before they launch into a longer project (fan fiction, anyone?). Casual dating is great for the same reason—maybe you're fresh out of a relationship and not quite ready for something new, or you're trying to find your personal dating MO before you go all Ted Mosby and start looking to meet your future kids' mother. Or maybe you just want to have some fun without worrying about plotting out the next ten years of your romantic life.

If this is the case, and you aren't ready to put a label on it, casual dating might be best for you. You still need some me time, and it isn't fair to get involved with someone who wants to go all in when you're not ready for that.

You're Experimenting

Just as RPing with different partners is all about trying new pairings to see what works, casual dating is about trying to find out who is right for you romantically. Maybe you've spent most of your dating life with decidedly geeky people, and now you want to try and see what happens if you date a non-geek. Perhaps all your previous relationships revolved around sitting on the couch and playing video games, and now you want someone who doesn't game at all. Or maybe this is your first foray into dating in general. Casual dating is about meeting new people and expanding your horizons.

You're interested in a variety of conversations.

In online forums, there's no limit to how many threads you can get going at once (as long as you can attend to them all). In dating, it's pretty normal to go on a few dates here and there with different people, especially if you're finding dates online. It's far easier, after all, to contact and talk to multiple people when you're dealing with online profiles, as opposed to having friends set you up.

THE CASUAL DATING RULEBOOK

If casual dating seems right for you, let's flip through the rulebook. Now, that's a bit of an exaggeration; there aren't any hard-and-fast *rules*, per se. Casual dating is more like a LARP than a tabletop game, in that there are a handful of simple conventions you should follow, and boundaries you should maintain, to make the experience successful and fun for all involved.

Rule #1: Don't go OOC. It's important to be honest, both about your character and about the fact that the relationship is casual. Honesty is key in this kind of dating (or any kind of relationship, in fact). You need to be absolutely clear about what is going on, to avoid hurting the other person. If you think this is a casual thang but she doesn't, you can bet the game is going to break. Conversely, if you're having a fine time bouncing from one encounter to another, you can't complain when you spot her having fun with some other player.

Rule #2: Agree on limits. Early in the game, when you agree that you want to keep seeing each other, you should get things out in the open and define how your shared universe is going to work. Who can cast spells? Is god-modding allowed? What are you going to call each other—friend? Friend with benefits? Partner in crime?

Rule #3: Be discreet. Okay, so you're dating other people, you're upfront about it, she's okay with it. That doesn't make it okay to go on and on to her about the other people you are seeing. After all, you don't drone about offstage activity in an RP (it's boring), so you shouldn't kiss and tell IRL.

Rule #4: Know your boundaries. This applies to both physical and emotional ones. Are you expecting to be in frequent contact with her, conversing often and connecting on a deeper level? Or do you expect that you won't communicate much when you're not out together? And what about sex—how comfortable are you with being intimate with someone you see only casually? While some people can disconnect the emotional link to sex, others can't. Make sure you're aware of your own boundaries, as well as hers.

There Can Be Only One: Exclusive Dating

Making the jump into an exclusive relationship is like making the jump to hyperspace: without precise calculations, you end up floating home. A lot of guys feel this way, and not all of them are interstellar smugglers.

But the truth is, transitioning from casual dating to something more committed often seems like a natural progression more than a leap into a non-Euclidean universe. When things go well, you reach a point in the relationship when neither of you is seeing anyone else, but you might not be calling each other "boyfriend and girlfriend" yet either. You might pass through a "short-term relationship" phase, as referenced in Chapter 1, that is more committed than casual but may not be completely exclusive. Or you might accelerate right into more serious maneuvers, like sharing root passwords or having a joint Xbox Live account. Dating exclusively can make people feel more secure, safe, and socially accepted. Plus, you get to stop taking that awkward pause when introducing your significant other to someone ("this is my . . . my . . . er, friend . . .").

Some couples have on-again, off-again exclusive relationships, while others jump in and become exclusive couples after less than a month of dating. Really, it all depends on the wants and needs of the people involved. As always, communication is a must. If you're starting to think about moving from an occasional team-up to a regular partnership, the thought has probably crossed her mind too. Which means it's time to open a hailing frequency and start the dialog.

But *how* you transmit the "will you be my girlfriend?" message isn't necessarily an easy thing to do. So that you won't be tempted to communicate via Elvish runes or tlhIngan Hol, here are some options.

You're not dating anyone else:
"It seems like we're both in this alone together. Let's make it official."

You find yourselves spending most of your free time together. You game together, you shop together, you go out to eat together:
"I'm pretty psyched I get to spend so much time with you. Can I do it as your boyfriend?"

You're happy doing decidedly non-date-ish things (loafing around the apartment, etc.):
"You make even the boring parts of my life awesome. Can I keep you around?"

You've been together for an extended period of time:
"I can't believe we've been dating for X months already. Do you think it's time to make it official?"

You seldom notice other people anymore:
"You're all I've been thinking about these days—not in a creepy way, I swear! Just in a . . . do-you-want-to-be-my-girlfriend way?"

HANDLING YOUR DIFFERENCES

No matter how perfect a couple might seem, there's always going to be some kind of ground that the two of them don't stand on together. That is to say, ground that isn't common.

Here's the thing. Differences can keep things exciting, as long as they are small and aren't what Liz Lemon refers to as "deal breakers." They can strengthen a relationship—and if you're moving into an exclusive dating situation, you obviously believe the relationship is worth strengthening. So think of the differences between you as the colors in Magic: The Gathering, and your relationship as the deck. According to Wizards of the Coast, the colors in Magic are driven by different values:

- White: Order. Protection. Light.
- Blue: Knowledge. Manipulation. Illusion.
- Black: Darkness. Ambition. Death.
- Red: Freedom. Emotion. Impulse.
- Green: Growth. Instinct. Nature.

The differences in the color traits are abundantly evident. White values order while red values freedom. Black focuses on death while green is all about growth. Blue seeks knowledge while red is more about impulse. And while some of these differences are pretty damn extreme, they also complement each other well. If your deck is all about healing and protection, how do you deal with damage and attack? If all your cards focus on illusion and manipulation, what protects you from physical forces? You certainly could play with a single-color deck, but a dual color deck is generally the way to go. (Tricolor decks do exist, but they can be tough to handle. And I'm not about to get into three-person relationships, Player One. What kind of a book do you think this is?)

Here are some quick tips for dealing with the inevitable differences that arise as you construct the deck that is your romantic relationship.

Recognize your complementary colors. Many geeky pursuits often complement another. Movies and comic books (how many comics eventually are *made* into movies?), video games and the outdoors (maybe play some Wii Sports?), science fact and science fiction . . . The things that make you different can often bring you together.

But what if your differences are deeper? Again, think back to those opposing colors in Magic: The Gathering: opposing traits can make for a winning combination when brought together. If you're naturally reclusive and shy and she lives to socialize, occasionally let her charisma help bring you out of your shell, while you in turn show her the value of some rejuvenating downtime. If you're spontaneous and she lives to plan, channel both your traits at the same time by scheduling a specific time once a week to do . . . whatever you decide at the last minute. And if she's a rock-solid pragmatist while you're an up-in-the-air dreamer, congratulations: you've got a well-rounded partnership that can handle almost problem that comes your mutual way.

Cut out what isn't necessary. Maybe you're clashing over differences that are petty and don't really matter in the long run. That ridiculous poster you've got hanging up in your bedroom, a certain outfit she keeps wearing that you loathe, little habits that you can easily rid yourself of (taking photos of everything you eat, for example)—these are easy to change.

Think about your Magic: The Gathering deck: way over 60 cards, piling up to, I don't know, let's just say 80. You want to get it to a lower number for maximum playability, so what do you cut out? The stuff you don't really need. That artifact creature that costs 10 colorless mana that you keep around because it looks cool. Or those four enchantments you have, even though you only really need two. It can sometimes be a painful step to take, both in life and in Magic, to cut out the little unnecessary things. But after you do it, chances are you won't even realize they are gone.

Learn to compromise. This can be pretty damn difficult, but really, the art of the compromise is what relationships are built on, whether it's you and your sweetie or the United Federation of Planets. In Magic, compromise is a key deck-building moment, when you rationalize, "If I take out *this* card, I can also keep *this* one." Or "If I remove these two creatures, I can keep this specific sorcery spell." Both people in a relationship need to realize that taking some cards out of the deck lets you bring new things to the table. You might have to miss your Tuesday night guild raid on WoW, and she might have to shave a few hours off her nonstop work life. But the result is that you enjoy more time *together*—and that's the whole point of a relationship.

The Togetherness Effect

So now that you and Player Two are together, you may reach a point where you're really *together*—eating, sleeping, gaming, breathing, and everything in between (if there's even anything left in between). The thing is, while spending every waking hour together might not ruin a relationship, it'll definitely drive you a little crazy—not to mention complicate your nonromantic social life. It's important to establish some boundaries that allow you both to enjoy time apart from one another.

MANA DRAIN

Be alert for these downsides of spending too much time together.

Ignoring Your Friends (-25 to Social Status): Everyone has experienced this: a friend in your social circle meets someone special and then practically vanishes. Much like Chef in that episode of *South Park*, when he's taken over by Veronica (a woman who turns out to be a succubus), your pal disappears and is consumed by his new relationship. While your crew will understand that you need alone time with your sigoth—especially in the early throes of a burgeoning romance—a mature relationship should leave you time to hang with your buds.

Running Out of Things To Talk About (-50 to Speech): Unless you're the Most Interesting Man in the World, you've got a limited number of amazing stories you can tell before you don't have much more to say. And if you're spending all your free time with your significant other, what are you going to have left to talk about once she's heard about all your past adventures? Spend some time apart, with friends, family, coworkers, whoever. Doing stuff on your own allows you to generate new stories to share with her.

Feeling Smothered (-50 to Personal Space): It doesn't matter how much you adore each other. Even if you're a couple that has more tolerance for simultaneity than most, eventually spending all that time in each other's quantum fields will leave one or both of you feeling smothered. And not in the delicious way that Pocky is smothered in chocolate and pure happiness—smothered in the "Okay you need to leave me the hell alone" sort of way. That's anger and resentment that doesn't need to be there, Player One.

The Risk of Codependence (-100 to Personal Identity): In any relationship, you should be able to depend on your partner. In fact, there are tons of stories revolving around that very concept. Superheroes, grizzled detectives, action heroes, even bad guys—plenty of them rely on some sort of sidekick. However, you still need to be able to function on your own. Robin, the quintessential sidekick, went on occasional solo missions and eventually became Nightwing, a crimefighter in his own right. I hope you and your Batgirl stay partners, Player One, but if you end up going solo you want all your skills to be intact.

1-UPS

Consider the following upsides of spending time apart.

Missing Your Significant Other (+50 to Fondness): Yes, the "absence makes the heart grow fonder" thing is a tired cliché, but clichés wouldn't exist if there weren't some underlying truth to them, right? Such is the case here. Spending time apart from your significant other gives you the chance to actually miss having her around. You won't take her for granted.

Reflection Time (+25 to Appreciation): I'm not talking about any of that inward journey, finding-your-center-with-a-penguin-in-an-arctic-cave-in-*Fight Club* sort of stuff here. Having time to yourself gives you the opportunity to think about your current status, what's working, and what might be missing. It's a great way to reflect on what you really want.

Better Lovin' (+150 to Libido): When you're away from your significant other, you don't just miss her emotionally. You miss her physically. You ache and yearn and all that romance novel stuff. So it's no surprise that when you're apart for a little a while, sex gets better. Don't be afraid to spend more than a day apart. A few days visiting family, a weekend road trip with the guys, a week-long business trip—these are all opportunities for an epic reunion.

BREAKING ORBIT

Three ways to add healthy space to your relationship.

Have separate hobbies. You don't need to drop the hobbies you enjoy together, but you should have one or two pastimes that she's totally not into (and vice versa). If both of your hobby sets completely overlap, each of you should take up something new.

Make plans with friends. Try to set up a recurring get-together, like a weekly lunch or twice-monthly movie outing. If you can't get your schedules to sync up on a regular basis, make sure you end every meet-up by planning the next one.

Schedule some alone time every day. It could be an early-morning jog, or a stop for coffee on the way home from work, or a 3 p.m. break to catch up on a favorite podcast. Maybe it's an unstructured hour that you can use for solo gaming, Internetting, or just hanging around eating pizza rolls in your underwear. Make a bit of me time part of your regular routine.

Dealing with Outworlders: Introducing your Significant Other to Your Friends

So you're ready to introduce your special someone to your peeps, and you're a little bit nervous. That's totally understandable. You want to avoid disrupting your group of friends—and at the same time, you want your girlfriend to be comfortable with them.

But relax. Adding another member to your social circle is a lot like adding an additional character to your party in a good RPG—and you know what that means, right?

BE CERTAIN SHE IS READY

In some games, like action/adventure titles, you have the opportunity to take on a new party member at any time. You'll meet them in a little town or out in the wilderness, and they'll be ready to join you when you're ready to have them.

But in other cases, the time may not be quite right. Maybe the upcoming mission is too dangerous, or you're simply not ready to have someone else with you at this point in the game. Similarly, before bringing your significant other to meet your friends, talk to her and make sure she is ready to meet them. If the situation doesn't seem right (a special friends-only party, for example), then reconsider. Try bringing her to a different event later on.

MAKE SURE SHE'S PREPARED FOR BATTLE

When you add a new character to a party in an RPG like Final Fantasy, the first thing you do is check their armor, weapons, and the various accessories that will help make them stronger and more defendable.

Prepare your significant other the same way you would a character in a game. Not with actual weapons and armor, mind you (unless you're going LARPing), but with the same ideas in mind: for defense, let her know any topics she should avoid talking about. For weapons, offer some ideas for how she can break the ice with your homies.

INTRODUCE YOUR NEW CHARACTER

In many modern games, socializing your character with the rest of the party is a useful tool for advancing their stories and learning more about them. (See the Mass Effect series for a great example.) It unlocks valuable dialogue trees that keep the game engaging. So don't forget to *introduce* your significant other to your friends, and stick around to facilitate conversations. Don't leave her feeling awkward and isolated while you gab the night away with some jerk you met at a *Game of Thrones* viewing party.

Transform and Roll Out? Merging Your Geek Life and Your Love Life

In relationships, two people come together to form something new, something that's more than the sum of its parts. This is a notion you're probably quite familiar with, Player One. After all, the geek canon includes muchos examples of robots and mechs joining to create bigger and more powerful constructs (not to mention the concept of a sentient piece of machinery Rubiks-cubing itself from one shape into another—there isn't a single self-respecting geek out there who isn't familiar with *Transformers*).

Now, as fun as it may be to think about you and your girlfriend uniting your interests into some unstoppable *Voltron* meets *Transformers* meets *Power Rangers* mash-up, combining forces isn't always so straightforward. Making your geek life and love life combine into one superbeing isn't as easy as clicking a few pieces into place.

As you're trying to merge your geek life and your love life, it's important to remember you can't force the person you're dating to connect with your interests in the exact way that you want her to. If you're an autobot and she's an aerialbot, you can't expect her to suddenly transform into a ground-based vehicle. But you can still bond over your mutual love of administering beat downs to Decepticons. Be respectful, be patient, be open to learning about *her* pastimes. And be realistic: it isn't the end of the world if your new love isn't 100 percent invested in your geeky passions. Remember, you are more than your hobbies.

With that in mind, here are three geektastic activities that you can easily make more couple friendly—whether she's a n00b who's game to try or a she-geek eager to expand her event horizon.

HACKING AND BUILDING TOGETHER

Romance and hacking electronics have gone hand in hand since the days of *Hackers*, *Tron* (the original!), and *War Games*. And working on some sort of gadget together creates opportunities for the two of you to geek out with others, as well as spend time one on one on doohickey. Following are some suggestions.

Visit your local hackerspace. The standard hackerspace is a community-driven place where people who love technology, science, and digital art meet up to collaborate and build fun, innovative projects. And most of these spaces host wonderful community events, inviting people to take classes, listen to lectures, and free-build their own projects. Don't be intimidated—you won't walk into a room that looks like it belongs in *Swordfish* or *The Matrix*. While some hackerspaces can be found in machine shops or open technology labs, they can also work as pop-up spots, appearing in libraries, at colleges, and even in bars.

It's a simple and generally inexpensive (depending on those classes, of course) way to have a geek date that shows off your interest, let the two of you share an experience, and give you plenty of chances to get close. You'll need to huddle together as you build that little Arduino robot, after all. If you're having a hard time locating a hackerspace in your area, try the Hackerspace.org public wikis. Chances are if there is a hackerspace in your area, it'll be listed.

 Fabrication spaces, or "fab labs," are much like hackerspaces, places to build things in a community setting—only fab labs focus on digital fabrication.

Check out a coworking space. Similar to hackerspaces, coworking spaces are where freelancers and artists get together to work in a social environment. While going on a work date might not sound very appealing (it isn't), attending an *event* at one these venues is a great idea. The people in these kind of spaces often are busy building new technologies and launching startups, but they also do plenty of community outreach. You're quite likely to find an excellent event connected to one, where people share some of the bold, creative new projects they're working on. These kinds of gatherings are bursting with great conversation starters and let your date know what you're about.

Attend a MAKE meetup. If you don't want to be limited to select spaces, like a coworking space or a hackerspace, you might want to check out a MAKE meetup—inspired by *MAKE Magazine*, the legendary publication that promotes DIY projects—where all kinds of people get together to work on fun projects in their backyards, basements, and garages. These are great events for socializing with fellow geeks, introducing your date to your geeky world, and maybe getting ideas for a project the two of you can start together.

GAMING TOGETHER

We geeks love sharing our passions with other people. We've already talked about the joys of cosplaying and cobbling together awesome robots. But what about sharing video games with your significant other? Sure, a lot of video games are meant to be played by one person and one person only. You can't exactly share an *Elder Scrolls* single-player campaign experience (well, you can, but we'll talk about that later), but there are plenty of other options available for couples who want to game. Is there any better way for the two of you to learn to work as a team and watch each other's back? Here are a couple of tips on making that happen.

Ask yourself: multiplayer or single player? If you want to game with your significant other, it's important to choose something you can both play and enjoy together. A single-player campaign in, say, an epic RPG isn't terribly fun if you're the spectator. Think back to when you were a kid and you had to watch one of your friends play through a single-player video game while you waited for your turn. Not exactly entertaining, right? Nevertheless, some couples *do* share single-player campaigns together, so this rule can be broken as long as you come to a consensus on this before popping the game into the console. Some people don't like sharing their saves; there's nothing wrong with that.

Match her skill level. If your GF doesn't know fragging from lagging, introduce her to gaming with something more n00b-friendly: Wii sports games, "sandbox" titles like Harvest Moon or Animal Crossing, or a quick bout of button-mashing beat-'em-up in Super Smash Bros. are all good choices for a first round. On the other hand, if you're both serious gamers, opt for something that will challenge you both (maybe this is your chance to finally figure out that game you can never beat). As long as the game isn't too easy, when it's over you'll feel like you've accomplished something together. And as a couple, that's a great feeling.

Don't over-game. It's easy to get lost in a good MMORPG with your significant other, raiding away together in a game of *World of Warcraft* hour after hour. But remember the importance of actual human interaction. There's a reason some online games have a built-in "You've been playing for X hours, please take a break" message that pops up after a while. Don't let your ability to communicate with other humans break down because you're spending too much time in the virtual world. Go out! Get some air!

Note: All of these rules apply to other kinds of games as well: D&D,

board games, collectible-card games like Magic: The Gathering, tabletop games like Warhammer 40,000. In a nutshell: make sure the game is friendly for multiple players, pick something suited to each of your ability levels, and don't overdo it.

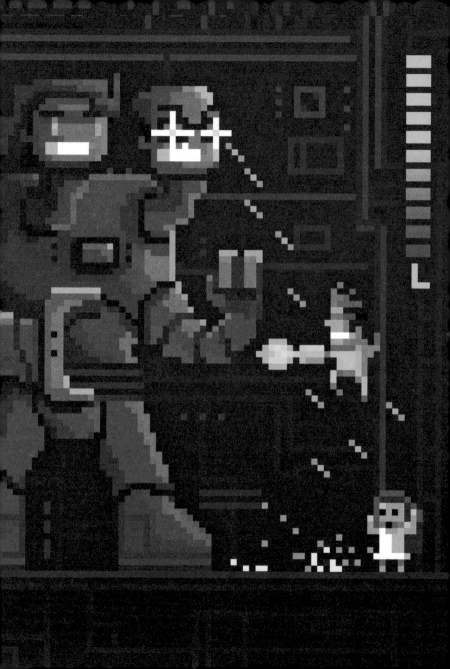

CHAPTER 7

Boss Level: Advanced Geek Dating

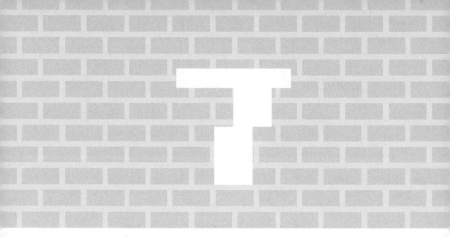

 ome very far you have, Player One. (Sorry, I mean, you have come very far. I don't know why I used that weird syntax.) Congratulations and well done and yadda yadda yadda.

However you find yourself getting into a relationship, eventually you'll reach a point where (to quote Led Zeppelin) there are two paths you can go on (in the long run). Things can get serious, in which case you'll move towards shared life goals (family, kids, pooling your funds together to purchase that rare *Spider-Man* variant you've always dreamed about). Or you can move towards an eventual break up. Endgame. Game over, man!

So put on the *Final Fantasy VII* soundtrack and blast "One Winged Angel." It's time for the ultimate boss battle. The Sephiroth of relationships. In this final chapter, we'll explore both paths that lie before, and how you should navigate each of them.

THE TRUTH IS OUT THERE: SIGNS THAT THINGS ARE SERIOUS

So you're in an exclusive dating situation. Is it, you know, *serious*? Well, if someone close to you (a family member, friend, or coworker) responds to news of your girlfriend with a remark like "wow, sounds like it's getting serious," then congrats—things probably are getting serious.

However, if no such helpful statement has been made, and you're as oblivious to your relationship status as Yorick is in *Y: The Last Man*, here are a couple of very clear signs that yes, your relationship is getting serious:

● **You have a routine.** While repetitious rituals can make a relationship grow stale and boring, there's nothing wrong with a couple having some comfortable, predictable, yet mutually pleasant routine behaviors. Maybe you both go get comics together on New Book Day, or you both love waiting in line together for a midnight video game release. Maybe Thursday night is Pizza Night. Maybe *every* night is Pizza Night, and you've both memorized each other's favorite toppings. Those kinds of fun, even mundane customs are an inevitable part of couplehood. They become nice little pleasures you can count on no matter what else is going on in the space-time continuum. And they're definitely a sign things are getting real. Fasten your seatbelt.

● **You don't plan to spend time together.** When you first start seeing someone, you generally make a lot of plans in advance. Once you start staying over at each other's places at night, making each other breakfast, and continuing on with your days together . . . bam. Serious. You're no longer making active attempts to hang out. You're just *doing it*. It happens

automatically, like Wolfwood showing up in whatever godfor-
saken town Vash the Stampede wanders into.

- **You've had your first real fight.** It doesn't matter how perfect
they seem: all couples fight. And the *reason* they fight, at least
partly, is that they place great value on the connection they
have and don't want to give it up without a, well, you know.
If the two of you have had at least one verbal slugfest, full of
combo moves and special attacks, but it didn't deal a finishing
blow to the relationship...clearly you both feel you have something worth holding on to.

- **You're in constant communication.** Do you text each other
through the day, or call each other just because? Those little,
daily efforts that let your significant other know you're thinking
about her are a classic signal that you're in it for the long haul.

- **You've dropped the L-Bomb.** Hopefully you aren't as clueless
as Scott Pilgrim is when Wallace is trying to have a talk with
him about using that precious four-letter word. Have you been
using the word "love" in your relationship, and have those feelings been reciprocated? Well then, this *is* serious.

FORWARD COMPATIBILITY: FIGURING OUT COMMON VALUES

As great as it is to get comfortable with being serious in a relationship, once you're there, it's important to look ahead. Your rapport as
a couple might be fantastic, your chemistry explosively awesome, and
your interests—be they bad movies, good video games, White Castle
at two in the morning, or some combination of all three—as *in common* as they are *uncommon*. But there's more to a long-term relationship than stuff like finding the perfect MMORPG to play together (and
not just because MMORPGs close. I feel bad for couples who met in
City of Heroes, *Shadowbane*, or *Star Wars Galaxies*).

Think of the Game Boy: it was worth hanging on to even after the newer Game Boy Color came out, because it had the capacity to handle the new GBC games. The same is true in relationships: things change, transitions happen, and you've got to know that your current framework will handle what's coming next. And while you may not know the exact nature of future releases, you probably have a sense of what's on the horizon—the kind of big, "let's-start-our-life-together" questions that you'll need to answer eventually.

Potential environments for software incompatibility include:

- **Emotional validation.** Forget Mars and Venus—you're both from Earth. But just because you share a home planet doesn't mean you necessarily share a common language of affection. How comfortable are the two of you with sharing your feelings? How can you make sure that each of you is getting appropriate appreciation from the other? Do you need to say "I love you" in person every day, or will your GF be okay with the occasional in-game kiss?

- **Physical attention.** In a serious relationship, one that's heading towards long-term and perhaps legally sanctioned commitment, sex is important. The two of you need to be happy with your sex life. A lack of physical intimacy, or intimacy that isn't making one half of the couple happy, can lead to game-breaking resentment and dissatisfaction. Just like in a good game of D&D, the *dialogue* is what moves the action forward. If something isn't working for you, then you need to speak up about it. And be clear! If you say "I kind of think I might want to cast magic missile," the DM isn't going to get it—or worse, think you said "Tenser's floating disc." Not the same thing at all.

- **Intellectual connection.** You don't need to be debating the philosophical underpinnings of *The Matrix* with her for hours on end. But for relationship longevity, you should be able to have a good, engaging discussion or two with your GF—even if it's just about how bad the sequels were.

Trust and faithfulness. Is this a person who you can depend on? Does she keep to promises you agree on, and respect your opinion when you disagree? If you were about to be frozen in carbonite and she said "I love you" but you just smirked and said "I know," would she, despite your devilish air of insensitivity, find a way to thaw you out? Important questions, all.

Sharing finances. Who's going to lay down the plastic for Xbox Live? What about the weekly pizza run? Are you the sort of person who is okay sharing your finances with your significant other, or do you prefer to have a separate bank account, credit cards, etc.? Both of these options are okay, but both definitely require a conversation.

Religion. It's sometimes easy to overlook faith-based differences when you're in the throes of sexy geek passion. But when you're thinking about starting a life together, there is definitely a Serious Conversation about it on the horizon. How big a role does faith play in your life together? Is it okay if you worship at the First United Church of the Fonz while she attends the Church of Ned Flanders? Will you pray together to the Flying Spaghetti Monster or will the Ron Swanson Pyramid of Greatness determine your moral compass?

Settling down. If you want to stay where you are for the rest of your life, and your significant other plans to volunteer for the first civilian space colony (or even just move to a different city), you might run into some serious problems. Think about how you will (or won't) handle being apart if that's on the horizon (unless you can go in together on one of those futuristic virtual reality holodecks from Ray Bradbury's "The Veldt"—that would be wicked awesome *and* it would solve your problem).

● **Getting married.** There are plenty of creatures, both real and fictional, that mate for life: swans, bald eagles, penguins, griffins, vultures, albatrosses, termites, and even certain species of worms. Most humans are no different.

Still, you're not a worm, Player One. While those creatures are all pushed along by instinct, we humans are moved by emotion and personal desires. Marriage isn't for everyone, so it's important to have a talk about it at some point when your relationship starts getting serious. If one of you really wants to get married and the other has zero interest in the fellowship of the ring, something's gotta give.

● **Having kids.** Do you want perpetuate your genes through the traditional *Homo sapiens* reproductive process? Adopt a child found in a crashed rocket ship? Foster some mutants who found their way out of the subterranean city? Or would you be

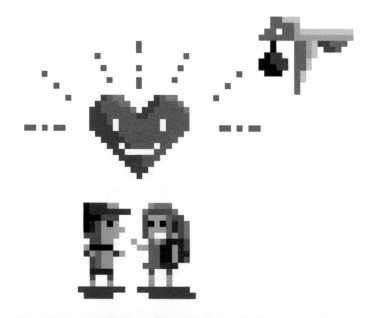

satisfied with some guinea pigs and your precious, precious
freedom? Whether or not to raise some younglings can be a
major deal breaker if the two of you don't agree.

SHARING YOUR FORTRESS OF SOLITUDE: MOVING IN TOGETHER

A geek's home is his castle, and when the princess decides to move
in, she's bound to change things (and I don't just mean the sheets
you haven't washed in months).

Bringing in someone to share you space and your stuff is a big
deal, so there are a few things to keep in mind *before* you move in
together. Here's a little checklist to help you consider whether or not
you're ready to open your lair to an outlander (or start a colony on
her moon).

- **You're both sure.** Cohabitation can be complicated enough
  with non-romantic roommates (please see the show *Being
  Human*, where a werewolf, a ghost, and a vampire share a flat),
  so it's important to make sure you and your GF are invested in
  this. Sharing a home is a real investment—of money, of time,
  and of *stuff*. Don't do it just because "it seems like the next step"
  or "all our friends have already done it." If either of you have
  doubts, your relationship should be able to handle a longer wait.
- **You enjoy each other's company.** If you're moving in together,
  it's vital that you know how to have fun with each other—and
  not just when you're going head-to-head in Halo, either. Living
  together means enduring all the boring things like grocery
  shopping, bill paying, and arguing with your landlord . . .
  together. Are you up for it?
- **Your lifestyles sync up.** Do you spend a lot of time staying up
  really late, playing video games, while your significant other

likes to hit the hay early? Or do you wake up before the crack of dawn while she stays up late? And what about your top-secret double life of taking to the streets as a masked avenger to fight crime? Strategize early for ways to work around each others' schedules—don't wait until it becomes a problem.

- **You spend most of your time together already.** If you can't get enough of your significant other, to the point where she is constantly sleeping over and seldom at her own place (or vice versa), then it just makes sense to merge fortresses. Less time shuttling back and forth means more time for togetherness.

- **You want the same things.** As long as you both want the same things in the relationship (see above), moving in can work out fine. However, if one of you doesn't really see this as something that'll move the relationship forward . . . well, you're going to run into trouble.

- **You've already had a fight.** When you're living with your sweetheart, you won't be able to just slam the door and run away after an argument. Because *you live together.* Friction is inevitable, so before you cohabitate, make sure you're able to resolve arguments, even big, loud, angry ones, via communication and compromise.

- **You've gone on vacation together:** Can you travel well together? All those hours of trip planning, ticket booking, suitcase packing, and really boring highway driving add up to a good trial run to evaluate a potential living-together arrangement.

WELCOME TO THE MOTHERSHIP: DEALING WITH YOUR GIRLFRIEND'S FAMILY

There's a reason origin stories are such a big deal in the geek canon: where you came from has a lot to do with who you become. Meeting your significant other's family is a pretty huge deal, a window into her past and perhaps a glimpse into your mutual future (lots of us become our parents when we get older, after all). She knows all this, which means she won't take this first contact lightly. It's sort of like interfacing with an alien race for the first time. One false diplomatic step and the universe could be forever changed.

Okay, so maybe that's a bit dramatic; unless your SO belongs to the House of El, you probably have at least a species in common with her parents. But the stakes are almost as high, and the rules for interaction are pretty similar. When it comes to First Contact with parents, you want to be more like Elliott in *E.T.*, and not like Dutch in *Predator*. So:

- **Know what you can and can't talk about.** Do some recon with your GF about topics that you should avoid. Even if you've been seeing one another for a while, there's always the chance that there are a few things in her family history that you're not aware of. What if her aunt is racist, or her cousin thinks *Star Wars* Episodes 1–3 are *good*, or her mom is one of those aliens from *Signs* that dissolves on contact with water? Everyone has *that* family member. Be prepared.

- **Emphasize your humanity.** While your girlfriend's family might not see you as the "man" in *To Serve Man*,* they *are* going to see you as the man in her life. So tell them some solid, trustworthy facts about yourself—a casual mention of your steady job, respect for their daughter, or encyclopedic knowledge of emergency first aid. Let them know that you're

---

*Which is good, because To Serve Man *is actually . . . no, I won't spoil it.*

- not the alien life form in this movie. Better yet, *show* them with a thoughtful host gift or an offer to help out.
- **Don't play xenolinguist.** Her uncle knows the ins and outs of the latest Omnibus Blah Blah Bill making its way through Congress. And you? In the last election, you wrote in a vote for Admiral William Adama. On our Babelfish-less planet, some words really do go in one ear and out the other. Resist the urge to fake your way through a conversation about unknown matters, no matter how eager you might be to jump in. The last thing you want is to end up looking foolish in front of your significant other's family when you get dumped out of the conversational airlock with no helmet. Participate by asking questions, nodding thoughtfully, and steering things back to topics you're familiar with.
- **Be polite.** No matter what weird situation you get into, a friendly smile and an affable attitude go a long way. Resist the urge to go all *War of the Worlds* and panic if an uncomfortable conversation starts to escalate. Don't succumb to troll bait, don't engage in a flame war, and let polite disagreement be your response to the most upsetting of statements. Whatever happens, your girlfriend will be grateful for your accommodating nature.

I've Got a Bad Feeling About This: Breaking Up

In this section, we're going to talk about the worst part of a relationship (or the best, depending on who you're dating)—the end. It's not a pleasant topic. But luckily for you, Player One, there are endless lessons on this subject to be gleaned from pop culture. Because everyone loves watching a good breakup movie in their Zoidberg boxers while eating cookie dough ice cream through a straw…or maybe that's just me.

Speaking of which, let's consider the *Futurama* episode "Love and Rocket," in which Bender starts dating the spaceship that he and the crew use to deliver packages. The relationship is doomed from the start, for a number of reasons:

> ⯈ Bender is dating someone he works with.
> ⯈ The Planet Express ship doesn't listen to the advice of her friends (Fry, Leela).
> ⯈ Bender is into casual relationships, and the Planet Express ship wants something serious.
> ⯈ The Planet Express ship *is a spaceship*.

When Bender finally does decide to break up with the ship, he does so when the crew is under attack by a fleet of aliens called Omicronians. The ship's fragile psyche breaks, she stops in space, and gets blasted by missiles. Fry insists that Bender could have chosen a better time to break up with the ship. To which he replies:

"Ah, the moment felt right. Call me old-fashioned, but I like a dump to be as memorable as it is devastating."

Point being, Player One, this is totally the wrong way to end a relationship, particularly one so full of complications. Breaking up is tough. Not just on the person being broken up with, but the person doing the breaking up (does that make sense? If I call them the Dumper and the Dumpee, would that make it any clearer?). Don't underestimate its power.

END A RELATIONSHIP, SALVAGE SOME EXP

As your character learned in *Fallout: New Vegas* or *The Elder Scrolls V: Skyrim* (as well as subsequent and past titles), experience leads to growth. The more you jump and run, the better your agility gets. The more you shoot and fight, the stronger and more accurate you become. And the more you talk with people, the higher your speech rate gets.

So, what does this have to do with the end of a relationship? Pretty much everything.

When you find yourself in the unfortunate position of ending a relationship, you'll likely hear a lot of tired clichés from friends and family. More fish in the sea, don't give it up, etc. Try your best to ignore them, and focus on one thing:

EXP.

There's more to a relationship that having somebody around for a good time. Relationships are about growth, and growth is just the real-world version of Experience Points. Every important person in your life should help you grow, and the special someone that you're dating is no different. Though it might be tough to accept, every relationship that doesn't work out can turn into a learning experience. Looking back, you'll probably find that you've learned a lot about yourself. You've learned about your ability to deal with another person's foibles. You've learned what happens when you leave the toilet seat up in the middle of the night. And, most important, you've learned what you do and don't want out of a relationship.

So as painful a breakup can be, it's no Ragnarok. In fact, it may not even *be* a breakup. Answer me these questions three, before the other side ye see:

- **Are you sure you want to break up?** This might sound silly, but make certain you actually want this to be over. Did you just have a massive fight or major disagreement? If so, make sure there really is no way to compromise, apologize, or work through the problem. Also, don't be one of those people who use breaking up as a threat to win an argument.

● **Are you making a nonemotional decision?** Yes, when making a decision like this, you should search your feelings (you know this to be true). However, when you're upset or angry, it's all too easy to make a decision based entirely on emotion, instead of giving rationality a chance to chime in. Consider Bruce Banner; he gets angry, turns green, smashes things, and hurts those closest to him. The Hulk is a hero, but he's not admired for his decision-making prowess (especially when it comes to his choice of pants). If you're on the verge of Hulking out, take time to cool down and revert to Bruce status.

● **What about second chances?** Would you be willing to give your significant other a second chance? If your answer is yes, consider what it would take to fix the current relationship. Talk about these issues first, before you bring up a breakup. If it turns out that these problems really can't be fixed, then at least you'll know you tried.

Still sure you want to end the relationship? You've made a nonemotional decision and determined that yes, breaking up is the best thing for you? Maybe for both of you? Okay then, let's continue.

BREAKING UP: THE ULTIMATE STRATEGY GUIDE

Having your heart injured by shrapnel, requiring you to wear an arc reactor just to keep it beating? Meh, maybe a little inconvenient. But having your heart broken in the emotional sense? Devastating. It's bad, Player One. And not in a so-bad-it's-good *Starship Troopers* kind of way. I'm talking a genuinely-bad *Battlefield Earth* kind of way.

But there are ways to soak some of the damage. To start, try to make the experience as not-devastating as possible for the other person (despite what Bender B. Rodriguez says). Yes, you may be angry, hurt, depressed; you may even be the recipient of some undeserved nastiness from the lady on the other side of the screen. But avoid any childish, vindictive, or callous behavior, Player One. First, because you're a class act. And second, because you've got enough pain coming and you don't need the added sting of knowing you acted like an ass.

With that out of the way, let's delve into some key strategies for getting through this asteroid field with as little hull damage as possible.

Actions

Make it so. There's no sense in dragging out the whole process so it takes longer than necessary. Your breakup doesn't need to drag on as long as a Peter Jackson trilogy. Once you've made the decision, it's best to just go forward until you're out. The longer you take to do it, the more unhappy you'll be, and unfortunately, you'll end up taking all that out on your partner.

 Be aware, though, that *just do it* only applies after you've carefully considered if breaking up is the right move. The deliberation should take a while—but the up-breaking itself should not.

Choose the appropriate spacetime coordinates. Unfortunately, there is no magic place and time that will make a breakup hurt any less. But you can at least attempt to make the setting comfortable: Pick someplace private. Despite the clichéd advice to the contrary, choosing a public setting won't automatically stop her from being upset, crying, or yelling at you—even with all those stormtroopers watching, Leia *still* freaked out when Alderaan got blown up. Better to do the thing in a private space than surrounded by a bunch of slack-jawed gawkers.

Be wary of using non-in-person forms of communication. For short-term or casual relationships, breaking up over the phone is fine, especially if you think she'll go nutsoid on you. For anything longer, man up and do it face-to-face. And don't even think about doing this online.

As for the time, we're not talking about a time of day here. We're talking about an appropriate day that won't compromise the rest of her week. Does your soon-to-be-ex have an important meeting that day? A major exam? A piano recital? A work trip? It's okay to wait and spare her the emotional distress that might ruin something else going on in her life.

 Please, Player One, don't do the "we have to talk" thing and then not talk until way later. That just leaves her wondering what is going on until you do talk, and no one likes battling an anxiety attack all day.

Keep a steady course. No matter what you do, there's a good chance your now-ex will be upset with you. If your relationship has been full of fights up to this point, you might be in for a serious one right about now. Don't go Incredible Hulk on her. Don't even go Ang Lee's *Hulk* on her. Keep calm and carry on, my wayward son.

 Don't drown your anxieties with liquid courage, no matter how tempting a solution it may seem. A drunken tirade is the opposite of the quick, clean breakup speech you want—so hands off that mana potion.

Stay in the neutral zone. During a breakup, some couples are quick to throw in the suggestion that they remain friends, sometimes friends with benefits. At this point, before you've established a post-breakup lifestyle, it's incredibly important to know your boundaries. Otherwise you risk drifting back into the same orbit that made you so miserable. Some ex-couples can jump into a friendship right away. For others, it takes years to forge a friendly alliance. Friendship with benefits sounds fun in theory . . . but it could be her way of holding on to you (or vice versa). And you're likely to get confused or worked up emotionally. At the very least, spend some time apart before you try to establish a new kind of connection.

Maintain power to life support. Just because you're breaking up doesn't mean you can't show some tenderness. If she cries, don't push her away. If she gets angry, try to calm her down. Unless she's committed some kind of unforgivable act—and changing your ringtone to the theme from *Star Trek: Enterprise* doesn't count—you owe her something for the good times you had. This isn't the time to get up and run away. Breaking up is like redefeating all the bosses at the end of *Megaman*: it's painful and tedious, and it can get pretty damn ugly. But you need to see it through.

Dialogue

Don't talk in Klingon. Or Dwarvish, or Bocce. To put it another way: Be clear. No matter how you lead into it, you've got to get the basic message across: *we are breaking up*. Think old-school, text-based adventure games—the directives have to be short and direct to be understood, so don't be vague or coy in an attempt to cushion the blow (but don't start your breakup speech with *get lamp*, either).

Share your data. You need to explain yourself, Player One. If you're going to break up with someone, there has to be a legit reason why. Be honest, briefly explain your reasons, and be sensitive about it—no one likes to hear why they aren't wanted. Make your reasons about *you* (but don't resort to "it's not you, it's me"). If need be, make yourself a small list of reasons why it isn't working out, so you'll know what to say later on.

You should not, for any reason, actually use that list when talking to your soon-to-be-ex. It makes the situation all the more painful—and makes you look like a calculating jerk.

Disengage your cloaking device. You know how we just talked about being honest? That means avoiding clichés like the plague (see what I did there?). This is not a time to disguise your intentions by cloaking them in platitudes. You know what they are: "It's not you, it's me." "I love you but I'm not *in love* with you." "I have to go now. My planet needs me." Stuff like that. Be a grown-up and talk straight.

 Relationships with other people are all about growth, remember? If there was something seriously missing in your relationship, this is your chance talk about it. Give your partner a chance to grow from this experience, just as you hope to grow yourself.

WORST. BREAKUP. EVER.: HAZARDS TO AVOID AT ALL COSTS

Channel your inner Comic Book Guy and think about this for a second: what do you remember the most about movies or comic books? The ending, right? So would rather leave your ex with memories of a breakup you handled like the well-meaning mensch you are, or of the several miserable weeks you ignored her and acted increasingly douchey? Would you rather have an awesome ending that sheds light on everything that came before—like Charlton Heston's Statue of Liberty moment in the original *Planet of the Apes*? Or an eye-rolling, tediously predictable ending like Tim Burton's *Planet of the Apes*? (Or, for that matter, something that never seems to end when you want it to like *The Return of the King*).

Recall again that little gem from Bender in *Futurama*. It's a perfect example of what *not* to do. He cheated. He pushed her away. And in the end, he broke up with her at a horribly inappropriate time, hurting her feelings and risking the well-being of all his friends and colleagues. (Number one place not to break up with someone: In the cold vacuum of outer space.)

Fact is, there are a number of entirely inappropriate ways to handle a break up. Most of them involve acting like you're living in the *Star Wars* saga. You know how Yoda once said, "Do or do not, there is no try"? Well . . . DO NOT DO THESE THINGS:

- **Wait for the situation to collapse like the Old Republic.** While it might seem easier to just start distancing yourself from the person you're dating, in reality, just waiting around for your relationship to crumble apart on its own is a poor tactic. Denying intimacy, avoiding communication, and spending less time together isn't a good way to end things. Not only will your significant other question what's going on, she'll be left with bad memories of your time together, instead of good ones. And you know what else? It won't be much fun for you, either. The relationship's no good to you dead.

- **Cheat like a chess-playing Wookiee.** If you're unhappy in your relationship, cheating is a horrible way to instigate a breakup—it's the two-wrongs-don't-make-a-right equation that you learned in childhood. Not only does it ruin the memories of the relationship retroactively, it can complicate things with your social circle (people take sides in messy breakups like this!) and ruin your reputation. You know who cheats? *Cheaters*. Either break up or honor your commitment, Player One.

- **Use the Internet as your personal Death Star to attack her.** Resist the urge to blow up and vent on your networks, either before, during, or after your breakup. Everyone will see it, everyone will make judgments—not all in your favor—and everyone will know you're a loudmouth who doesn't know how to keep his dirty laundry in the hamper. Just update your status to single (or better yet, just leave yourself with no status whatsoever) and move on.

Spoil the ending like Homer Simpson walking out of ESB. Think of the epic nerdraging that's unleashed when someone slips the ending to, say, *Harry Potter* (spoiler alert: he's Voldemort's son!). Now imagine all that anger trained on you. If news of your intent to break up with your significant other reaches her inbox before you can talk about it, things get pretty ugly, pretty fast. Resist the urge to prepare everyone in your life for this breakup before it actually happens—talking it over with a close friend is okay, but blasting it out to everyone via text or Facebook isn't. It's tasteless, and you never know who might leak out your information.

Insist friends choose between Empire and Rebel Alliance. If you've been together a while, chances are the two of you have mutual friends. Don't take the low road and send out mass text messages or email chains, demanding everyone delete her from their life. Some of them may take your side, some may take her side, some may stay neutral . . . but that's up to them, not you. Insisting that your friends no longer speak to your ex will just make them angry and make you look small.

Send a breakup message via droid-projected hologram. We've been over this before, but it bears repeating: text messages, e-mails, tweets, Facebook posts, and the like are not acceptable formats for ending a relationship. Even handwritten letters, which might seem classy and old-fashioned, aren't appropriate. Remember when Bart wrote that letter to Mrs. Krabappel? "Dear Baby. Welcome to Dumpsville, population: You. P.S. I am gay." No matter how suave you might think your email is, it's always going to read like that letter from Bart.

- **Use a blaster instead of a more elegant weapon.** As upset as you may be, don't just blast away with every random complaint, irritation, criticism and insult in your arsenal. Think more lightsaber than blaster. Precise, not clumsy; relevant, not random. State only what you need to, then prepare yourself to block any return fire.

RECHARGING YOUR LIFE METER: HOW TO HANDLE GETTING DUMPED

Few things are harder than being on the receiving end of a bad breakup. You're left sad, confused, and feeling like your 8-bit heart was just shattered into tiny little pixels. Your life meter feels depleted, and you wonder how you'll ever be able to fill it back up again.

It's okay, Player One. This isn't a time for giving up. Never give up, never surrender, remember? Here are a few tips that'll help you move on, recharge, and handle the breakup properly.

- **Don't try to re-create the past.** When DC Comics announced that they were releasing a series of prequels to *Watchmen*, the comic book masterpiece, creator Alan Moore was understandably enraged: he wasn't the one writing them. He knew that this follow-up would compromise the legacy of the genre-changing opus he'd worked so hard to bring into being. If you sit around anxiously awaiting another go at a broken relationship, you might find yourself in a similar situation. Could a new version of something so great possibly be as good as the original? If it's a failure, or just a weak imitation of the first one, won't that color your memories of the initial experience?
- **Remember, relationships are a learning experience.** Once they're over, it's best to move on from the original and onto something new. Holding out for an unnecessary sequel usually

ends in disappointment (see *Indiana Jones and the Kingdom of the Crystal Skull* for a painful example. How long did we wait around for that?). In the end, a retread will only hurt more, even if you do have a refrigerator to hide in. (There's another movie franchise whose prequels not only failed to capture the magic of the originals, but were so incredibly disappointing that fans remain bitter to this day . . . but the name escapes me right now.)

Feel those feelings, human. As geeks, we prize rationality. And as dudes, we're supposed to deny we have any feelings at all. But complete emotional control is for Vulcans, not real-world human beings. (Besides, even Spock totally lost it now and then, and not only when it was Vulcan rutting season.) Let yourself be sad. Be angry! All too often after a break up, guys try to be tough, and conceal the fact that they are, in fact, hurting pretty bad. Keeping all that negative energy inside won't do any good, and you'll likely end up releasing it in a negative way that hurts people around you (that's how The Punisher got started). Try channeling the upset into something physical... maybe it's time to drag that mountain bike out of the basement and go find some actual mountains?

Purge yourself. No, I'm not talking about purging in the Allfather-in-*Preacher* kind of sense. I'm talking about the real-world equivalent of data purging: remove anything in your environment that reminds you of your ex. There's no sense in keeping all those pictures and mementos around; they'll only bring back painful memories. Put these things in a box and stash them someplace if you can't bring yourself to throw them away. And if you're deleting digital photos, make sure you actually delete them—don't just remove them from iPhoto like in *Forgetting Sarah Marshall*.

Activate the Cone of Silence. I understand how tempting the urge to give your ex a call or send an e-mail, text, or Facebook message is, Player One. But don't do it to yourself. It'll stress you out and make you upset, and not in the productive let-it-all-out-like-the-Hulk sort of way. Stay incommunicado.

Find distractions. If you need to, find some new hobbies that'll keep you from contacting your ex or brooding over your hurt too much. You've just ended something, so it's a good time to start something new. Maybe work your way through that backlog of games you've got sitting on the shelf. Or start following a new comic series. Write the screenplay you've been thinking about; enroll in the capoeira class you've always wanted to take; build the breakdancing robot you've been dreaming about. Anything that helps you focus on something positive and constructive is a good idea.

Spend time with your superfriends. Remember, you're avoiding contact with her, not with everybody else. Post-breakup misery is a classic "that's what friends are for" scenario. Just keep in mind that people don't always know how best to handle things when a friend is hurting; some in your social network may think you need some space. You may need to initiate contact, so don't let yourself become isolated.

Don't beat yourself up. This isn't the scene in *Fight Club* where Ed Norton smacks the hell out of himself in his boss's office. The urge to be tough on yourself about the decisions you've made is going to be tempting. In fact, it's almost unavoidable. The important thing is to not dwell on it—just as you did your best to treat her with respect during the breakup (right?), you need to by sympathetic to yourself, too.

A New Hope: When to Start Dating Again

Resurrecting from the death of a relationship is a lot like respawning after a bad date—but with more severe equipment damage. The key to getting back in the game is to take your time, check through your inventory, and make sure that everything in your arsenal's in working order before charging back into the fray. Here's a short list of what you'll need up and running:

- **Life meter:** Before you even think about dating again, make sure you're over your old flame and feeling good (see previous section). You can still be a little hurt, but make sure you're not hung up on her. Starting to date when you're still obsessing with an ex is unfair to anyone you might meet. Besides, you shouldn't jump back into a new relationship as a way to nurse your wounds—more than likely, you'll hurt a bunch of people (including yourself) in the process.

- **CPU:** Probe the depths of your psyche and think about what you're about to do. Are you thinking clearly about dating again? Are you doing it because you think you need to be in a relationship, or are you genuinely looking for something new? No one wants to be the rebound for someone just coming out of a relationship (unless she is also rebounding, making you a rebound, and then it's just layers upon layers like *Inception*).

- **Shields:** You're going to be feeling pretty damn sensitive once you're out of a relationship. You'll be the most emo kid ever, the equivalent of a mix tape loaded with the Get Up Kids, Dashboard Confessional, and the sappiest Something Corporate. You're the animated .gif of James Van Der Beek crying in *Dawson's Creek*. Get it? Good. The pain is only going to be worse if you try to date again before you're ready to deal with the possibility of being rejected.

Jetpack: Disable this bad boy. You don't want to rush into anything new right away. You're just out of a relationship, and you need to take it easy. No turbo boost, no hyperdrive, no boom tube. Just stay on impulse engines and see what's out there.

Map: Not just for where you're going, but for where you've been. You might feel like dating again is starting from square one, but in reality you've already unlocked plenty of rooms in the dating dungeon. And remember when we talked about the importance of meeting new character types for your party? Keep that in mind when starting to date again—and be smart about it.

Endings: A Final Note

When dealing with the concept of finality in geek culture, one finds there is ample wiggle room. Just when you think a super villain in a comic book is vanquished forever, he's resurrected a few issues later. Earth is destroyed? Don't worry, that was another dimension. You saved the princess? You won the game? Great! She'll be trapped in another castle in the sequel.

Remakes. Reboots. Resurrections. The geek canon, for better or worse, strongly encourages do-overs. Sometimes, these second chances give us something incredible. Like when Christopher Nolan resurrected the Batman franchise, the SyFy network brought back *Battlestar Galactica*, or Crystal Dynamics gave us the gritty, visceral relaunch of *Tomb Raider*.

Other times though, we aren't so lucky. We either get stuck with three attempts at a Punisher movie, or get halfway through an awesome reboot only to see it get canceled. (Sorry, *V.* You were too good for television.)

So when it comes time to reboot, restart, or just move on, remember to be patient, take it slow, and enjoy every exciting little moment that comes your way. After all, there is a wonderful thrill, a certain kind of rush, to watching something start over again, no matter how it ends. And in a new relationship, unlike games and certain movie franchises, you seldom find yourself living through the exact experience all over again.

Of course, the story doesn't *have* to end. Perhaps after careful reading and serious dating, you found that gal who makes you want to ignore the geek canon's obsession with starting things over. Why try to rewrite history if you're not in a *Crisis on Infinite Earths* situation (or the Flashpoint arc)?

If you're lucky enough to have found that special someone, I hope she becomes the Herminone to your Ron, the Rogue to your Gambit, the Pepper Potts to your Tony Stark. I hope she takes you by the hand and leads you through a door, the Ramona Flowers to your Scott Pilgrim.

And for those of you still questing . . . well, to quote *Galaxy Quest*: Never give up, never surrender.

Acknowledgments

If *The Geek's Guide to Dating* were an RPG, it would play a lot like *Final Fantasy Tactics: War of the Lions*.

Not because this book has a hidden battle system (or does it?), but due to the sheer number of characters involved. And if, as the writer, I'm the main character in this game . . . then all of these people would be in my party.

- **The Squires & Chemists:** To the party members who were there at the very start, ready to do battle, thank you for the early reads and valuable feedback. Especially Christopher Wink, Linzy Leon, Chris Illuminati, David Goodman, Jessica Anne Leon, Chris Urie, Steve Rauscher, Peter Marinari, Liz Crutchley, Tara Bennett, Kristin Hackett, and Cassandra Rose.
- **The Mages, Monks, & Mystics:** Gifted with mystical powers of editorial, design, sales, and production . . . the **entire** crew at Quirk Books.
- **The Orators:** Nicole De Jackmo and Mari Kraske, entering battle with their powerful voices. Thank you for making sure people heard about this book. And Kevin Nguyen and the Bygone Bureau, for sharing my essays about love and video games with the world.
- **The Bards:** To Robert LeFevre, Brian Johnson, and Adam Teterus, for singing the praises of comic books and subsequently making me obsessed, thus ruining me forever in the best way possible. Thank you for your invaluable notes and insight.
- **The Dragoons:** For constantly encouraging **me** to take big jumps, literary agent Dawn Frederick. And of course to Mom and Dad. For starting my game and helping me achieve my max level.

INSERT COIN TO CONTINUE

Or just visit quirkbooks.com/
geeksguidetodating to:

- ➤ Download other geek dating resources
- ➤ Get advice from geek dating guru Eric Smith
- ➤ Share your own geek dating story
- ➤ Exclusive videos of geeks in love
- ➤ and much, much more!